Bodysnatchers

Bodysnatchers

Digging Up The Untold Stories of Britain's Resurrection Men

Suzie Lennox

PEN & SWORD HISTORY

First published in Great Britain in 2016 by
Pen & Sword History
an imprint of
Pen & Sword Books Ltd
47 Church Street
Barnsley
South Yorkshire
S70 2AS

ISBN 978 1 78346 342 8

A CIP catalogue record for this book is available from the British Library

Typeset in 11/13 Ehrhardt
by Imago

Printed and bound in England by
CPI UK

Pen & Sword Books Ltd incorporates the imprints of Pen & Sword
Archaeology, Atlas, Aviation, Battleground, Discovery, Family History, History,
Maritime, Military, Naval, Politics, Railways, Select, Social History, Transport,
True Crime and Claymore Press, Frontline Books, Leo Cooper, Praetorian
Press, Remember When, Seaforth Publishing and Wharncliffe.

For a complete list of Pen & Sword titles please contact
PEN & SWORD BOOKS LIMITED
47 Church Street, Barnsley, South Yorkshire, S70 2AS, England
E-mail: enquiries@pen-and-sword.co.uk

Contents

Acknowledgements

Ever since I first encountered Britain's forgotten bodysnatchers whilst studying History as an undergraduate, I have always been surprised by people's curiosity when I mention this macabre topic. I am continually astounded by the number of people intrigued by the events played out in Britain's churchyards, in what has become known in some quarters as the 'Resurrection Times'. This interest has led to a number of collaborations which perhaps would not have occurred had it not been for the 'sack 'em up men' of England and Scotland.

There are many people without whose continued support this book would not have been possible. I'd especially like to thank Pen & Sword Books for their interest in bodysnatching and also thank my editors Jen Newby and Eloise Hansen, without whose support and constant patience this book would still be in the first rough drafts.

Thanks also go to the staff at the various archives who helped me unearth forgotten broadsides and for allowing me to share some of these finds with you. Special thanks go to the staff at Aberdeen Medico-Chirurgical Society, AK Bell Library, West Yorkshire Archive Service, Sheffield Archives and The National Archives, who have all been very helpful with my enquiries. A big thank you has to be said to Lynsey Halliday from the National Library Scotland, who has been patient throughout. Also to my former colleagues and friends at North Yorkshire County Record Office, who unearthed the letter from York School of Medicine much to my delight and have been a stream of constant support and enthusiasm throughout my research.

I am indebted to family and friends, especially Dr Kim Barker, who gave up much of their free time to explore Britain's abandoned churchyards and over-grown watch-houses with me. Some of the locations left a little to be desired and without the presence of a navigator I am sure I would have got lost on many occasions. I would also like to thank those involved for allowing me to get excited about another mortsafe or watchtower, for waiting for me to photograph every last one of them and allowing me to talk endlessly about bodysnatching!

Whilst writing this book I have tried to uncover the truth behind these long forgotten stories, many of which have now become part of the rich histories associated with the individual parishes, retold and embellished over the years. I would however be delighted to hear from anyone who has any further information on any of the cases mentioned throughout the book or to learn of new cases that I have yet to come across.

Preface

This book aims to put the record straight about Britain's resurrection men, to right the wrongs of muddled cases and to provide a voice for the forgotten bodysnatchers who stole cadavers from the grave and sold them to surgeons for a handsome fee. Many of the bodysnatching stories that have survived throughout the generations have been expanded from popular rumour or adapted and embroidered from newspaper reports; some an amalgamation of two or three stories.

This book unravels the snippets found in historical records and recorded in local legends, revealing the stories of the men – and women – involved in the macabre underworld of the bodysnatching trade. Churchyards and burial grounds the length and breadth of Britain were plagued by bodysnatchers from the mid-eighteenth century until the passing of the Anatomy Act in 1832. Many local cases have remained untold, hidden behind the better known stories of the Westport murderers Burke and Hare or Bishop, Williams and May, the 'Italian Boy' murderers.

The cases described within this book tell the stories of Britain's unknown bodysnatchers, highlighting the important part they played in providing cadavers for the dissecting tables of England and Scotland during the period.

Introduction

It is human nature to be inquisitive and medical students and physicians throughout history have proved no exception. Medical knowledge in the sixteenth century was still based on the theories of the Greek anatomist Galen (c.AD 130-200) and physicians and surgeons practised all types of medicine rather than specialising in one specific area. Therefore, it was perhaps inevitable that someone would eventually question Galen's philosophy and choose to study the internal organs of a human body, rather than those of a pig.

Galen had wrongly presumed that the organs of such animals were the same as the internal organs of humans. When early dissections were carried out, surgeons would refer to Galen's works. The internal organs of humans and animals, however, simply failed to match up. Any differences observed were put down to that particular human body being an inferior subject, rather than Galen having misread the variation in anatomy.

Galen's observations were beginning to be questioned in 1536/7 by the Belgian anatomist Andreas Vesalius. Often described as the 'Father of Modern Medicine', Vesalius acquired, by theft, the body of a condemned man from the gibbet. With this act Vesalius unwittingly set in motion among anatomists not only the desire to question what had gone before, but also the demand for a commodity that would not be adequately met for nearly 300 years.

The number of people interested in studying anatomy and wanting to enter the medical profession in Britain by the late eighteenth and early nineteenth century was then, as now, plentiful. The teaching facilities on offer were, however, somewhat lacking compared to those available on the continent. The universities of Leiden and Padua were the only establishments in which human anatomy was studied and this naturally drew students from over the known world, including Britain.

By the eighteenth century, students who had studied medicine abroad and returned to Scotland and England to become physicians and anatomists themselves, wanted to share the continental teaching methods with the new influx of medical students at home. Surgeons teaching in Edinburgh were allocated the body of one condemned man per year for the purposes of dissection, after a charter was granted on 1 July 1505 by the Edinburgh Town Council to the Incorporation of Surgeons and Barbers. In contrast, English surgeons were not permitted to use the bodies of condemned felons until 1540, when Henry VIII granted four cadavers annually to the United Company of Barber-Surgeons in London.

The paltry amount of five cadavers permitted annually for public dissection throughout Scotland and England perhaps initially slaked the thirst of the anatomists. Yet, it was not long before medical students and lecturers in England and Scotland became frustrated by the situation and decided to do something about it. In 1636, William Gordon, Mediciner at King's College, Aberdeen petitioned the Privy Council to be permitted to teach anatomy. He subsequently instructed the Provost, the chair of the town council, to provide two bodies of people who had died in hospital and whose relatives, if they existed, had failed to claim them.

Gordon's success resulted in sporadic applications from others for increased access to cadavers. In 1694, Edinburgh based anatomist Alexander Monteith successfully petitioned the Town Council to allow him the bodies of 'poor persons who die in Paul's Workhouse and have none to bury them'. The Edinburgh College of Surgeons, seemingly disgruntled by Monteith's new quota, also petitioned the Town Council for more cadavers and in November of the same year, they were granted 'the bodies of foundlings who dye betwixt the time they are weaned and their being put to school or trades'.

Surgeons in England, however, were not quite as fortunate as their Scottish counterparts. The United Company of Barber-Surgeons, created in 1540 by Henry VIII joining the Guilds of Barbers and Surgeons together was, by the late seventeenth century, slowly starting to divide. The surgeons were concentrating more on surgery, leaving the barbers to practice mainly bloodletting and tooth extraction. After failing to split from the barbers in 1684, the surgeons had to make do with the legal supply of six cadavers from the gallows per year, following an increase of two bodies provided by Charles II in 1663.

The feelings of the populace toward the medical profession at this time were shot through with fear, ignorance and disgust. In England, dissection was reserved for only the most depraved of criminals and would have been included as part of their sentence; their bodies being 'conveyed to the Surgeon's Hall for dissection' after hanging 'for the usual length of time'. The idea that dissection could be practised on a law–abiding parishioner who had recently been consigned to the grave was abhorrent. Any rumour or suspicion that the medical fraternity might be violating the graves of their loved ones could result in violent protest among the populace. The Christian belief that in order to be accepted into heaven your body had to be buried whole, also played an important part in making the act of dissection the most hated and feared act that the medical profession could carry out.

Nevertheless, the students and surgeons of Scotland and England wanted easier access to a greater number of cadavers and were beginning to consider illicit means of acquiring them. The different methods by which anatomists in England and Scotland acquired cadavers help to show the development of bodysnatching, from a task undertaken by reluctant students to a practice so widely spread, that unique preventative methods and resurrection techniques would develop across the country.

In England, whilst the London Company of Barber-Surgeons held the monopoly on the teaching of anatomy and lay claim to the sole legal supply of cadavers, some medical men were not adhering to the regulations laid down by the Company. The London anatomist William Cheselden (1688–1752) embarked on a series of private anatomy classes in 1711 from his home in Cheapside. He obtained cadavers by paying for bodies from the gallows, which had technically already been promised to the Company of Barber-Surgeons. When the Company went to claim their quota, they often found that Cheselden had got there first.

By 1714 the Company had had enough of Cheselden and forced him to close his doors to students. However, the idea and certainly the demand among students for additional tuition outside that offered by the Company of Barber-Surgeons, had been recognised. In just three decades, private anatomy schools throughout the capital would be dominating the teaching of anatomy in England.

In 1746, thirty years after the Company had forced Cheselden to close his doors to students, they made him Master of Surgeons within the Company. It has been suggested that his elevation to this position of authority indicates that private anatomy schools had been accepted, and in this role he was unlikely to go against the development of such establishments.

Although private anatomy schools had existed before William Hunter opened his school in London's Great Windmill Street in 1746, they were repeatedly closed down by the Company of Barber-Surgeons, as they were deemed to produce students ill-equipped to deal with the practices of surgery. With the Company aspiring to hold the monopoly on medical advancement in England, London was falling short in the range of anatomical training it offered to potential medical students. Students were beginning to head north to Edinburgh instead and, as a result, medical education south of the border was about to head in a new direction. With this movement of students, coupled with the prevalence of nepotism within the larger teaching hospitals, the rise in private anatomy schools in London occurred.

William Hunter's school on Great Windmill Street is perhaps the most famous of these early private anatomy schools. The anatomical collections amassed by Hunter's brother John form the Hunterian Museum, located at the Royal College of Surgeons in London today. Hunter had studied on the continent and was fuelled by the desire to teach anatomy in the 'Paris Manner', that is to ensure that each student had access to a cadaver. He offered his first course of anatomical lectures in 1746 and was richly rewarded for his enthusiasm, netting a profit of seventy guineas, the equivalent of nearly two years' wages for a craftsman, from this first series of lectures alone.

Great Windmill Street was not the only private anatomy school opened in London in the mid-eighteenth century and over the next few years even more schools would spring up throughout the capital. Although headway was being made in the private sector, it was not until Hunter advertised 'opportunities of learning the art of dissection. . . in the same manner as Paris' that people started to take notice of the private schools establishing themselves in the capital. The 'same manner as Paris' was the dream of every anatomy student, for they would be guaranteed a cadaver of their own to dissect. This was a world away from a demonstrator pointing out key features within the human body or watching as your fellow students hacked and stabbed their way through a thigh muscle.

By the mid to late eighteenth century, the advertising of anatomy tuition and 'chirurgical operations' was becoming more common throughout the country. In 1776 the *Oxford Journal* printed an advert for surgeon Mr Hunt advertising his 'anatomical and chirurgical lectures', which were to be held at his house in Burford, Oxfordshire for the course of six weeks at a cost of two guineas per course. Lectures would be held 'Mondays, Wednesdays and Fridays precisely at four o'clock'. Most importantly, however, was the availability of fresh cadavers for the duration of the course and Mr Hunt was promising:

> 'one body for dissections and another for operations, in every course. Dissections will be taught every Monday at three guineas and a half for each body, from six o'clock till eight. No expense or pains shall be spared to render this subject, which is to answer so extensive and so noble an end.'

The increased availability of instruction in anatomy and dissection classes providing each student with their own cadaver had one flaw: there were not enough bodies to go around. In order to keep the students interested and attendance at private lectures high, the lecturers and anatomists had no alternative but to become bodysnatchers.

Towards the close of the eighteenth century, private anatomy schools were continually favoured by medical students. After serving a seven-year apprenticeship, students still had to attend classes in human anatomy, and produce a certificate proving they had done so in order to become licensed surgeons. Students found that the private schools provided more opportunity for this requirement than the Company of Surgeons themselves. The private schools ran the same courses on anatomy as the teaching hospitals of St Bartholomew's, The London and the United Hospitals of Guy's and St Thomas's, but there was one crucial difference – they also provided the opportunity to dissect more bodies.

The increased growth of private anatomy schools in London was also occurring unchecked. No licence was required before a school could be opened and the ease of establishing them, combined with the demand from up-and-coming surgeons to attend anatomy lectures, meant that the schools were a complete success. The high numbers of students who attended Hunter's anatomy classes in Great Windmill Street reveal not only the need for these classes, but also the success of the new method of teaching morbid anatomy in England. Over a fourteen-week period, Hunter delivered '112 lectures for a student fee of seven pounds seven shillings and he frequently had a hundred students'. The attraction of fresh cadavers was clearly working and making some surgeons very rich indeed.

The introduction of 'An act for better preventing the horrid crime of murder' in 1752, more widely known as the Murder Act, helped to increase the number of available cadavers but only marginally. Under the new legislation it was to be at the court's discretion whether or not to grant the bodies of executed murderers to the surgeons for dissection and subsequent exhibition to the public. Furthermore, the Act made the attempted rescue of bodies from the surgeon's custody, subject to a sentence of seven years' transportation.

The passing of this act increased the anatomists' provisions by only between ten to thirteen cadavers per year, with the additional cadavers all destined for the Company of Surgeons. This was still woefully inadequate for the needs of the London anatomy schools, not to mention the needs of the private schools. Legislation had failed to keep up with the demand for improved medical training.

In response, bodysnatching intensified. In 1788 a doctor in London was charged with stealing the body of a woman from St Saviour's churchyard. The trial, Rex v. Lynn, was to be a turning point in the development of bodysnatching in England. Having turned a blind eye to the involvement of medical professionals in such a macabre operation, this case was to be a wakeup call to the authorities. Those surgeons who were involved in exhuming dead bodies had become, or so they thought, above the law and needed a reminder that what they were doing was not acceptable.

Three years before the Lynn case, on 14 October 1785, the bodies of four infants were stolen from St Andrew's Church, Holborn and taken to William Marshall's private dissecting academy at Thavies Inn. William Marshall was often found with cadavers that had been obtained by dubious means, but the men involved in this snatching were 'gentlemen' and the authorities were unwilling to prosecute because of their status. Yet, three years later, Marshall would again be charged with having two bodies in his possession.

The need to take action and curb this deliberate flouting of the law was becoming more evident. Lynn's case was considered a sharp reprimand to the medical community, yet the courts merely issued a lenient ten pound fine. Nevertheless, this warning was enough to make the medical professionals stop and think. The potential penalty of losing your reputation and subsequently your livelihood if caught stealing a cadaver was not a risk many surgeons were willing to take. The path was therefore clear for the professional resurrection men to embark on their trade.

Obtaining cadavers for anatomy classes involved a different procedure in Scotland than in England, but it was not altogether dissimilar. Within Scotland, Edinburgh lecturers were expected to supply cadavers for their students to work on, regardless of the number required, whilst students in the western city of Glasgow, were actively encouraged by their lecturers to go forth and exhume their own corpses. Although this book does not encompass the history of the development of medical teaching in Edinburgh, or Scotland as a whole, it is not possible to consider the development of bodysnatching without looking at the Monro dynasty.

The stories of Alexander Monro *primus* (1697–1767), Alexander Monro *secundus* (1733-1817) and Alexander Monro *tertius* (1773–1859) have been widely documented elsewhere, but they were pivotal in establishing the bodysnatching trade in Edinburgh. The first two generations perhaps unwittingly encouraged medical students enrolled at the University of Edinburgh to become bodysnatchers in their own right. Monro *primus* worked within the close confines of the law, using the officially allocated number of cadavers, regardless of the number of students he had in his dissecting room. Keeping body parts in tubs of brine, his dissatisfied students would rework arms and legs, fight over digits and limbs until there was nothing left to dissect, nothing left to learn from.

As anyone who has an enquiring mind knows, sometimes nothing can stop you learning and, as the commodity they needed was not available legally, the students acquired their own cadavers instead. Student involvement in exhumations was such a concern in the Scottish capital, that the Edinburgh College of Surgeons inserted a clause into indentures in 1721 forbidding apprentices to steal bodies or become involved in any exhumations. Glasgow students, meanwhile, were encouraged and even supported by their lecturers to provide their own cadavers for learning and perhaps due to this, there are more reports relating to Glasgow students and their bodysnatching exploits.

This 'entrepreneurship' and to some extent enthusiasm of the Glasgow students was not well received by the locals. The students were there to learn how to fix problems with the human body, to mend broken limbs and to carry out operations with the minimum of discomfort, they were not meant to be perfecting their bodysnatching skills.

The medical students' disregard for the morality of the activity they were embroiled in can be demonstrated by the frequency with which riots occurred throughout the city during the latter half of the eighteenth century. Glasgow University was assailed by an infuriated mob on a number of occasions in 1744, in 1748 and again in 1749, when a mob attacked the university after hearing of students involved in stealing cadavers for their studies. During the final riot, the militia was called for assistance, after students were believed to have targeted the Ramshorn Kirkyard. The mob was already at boiling point and nothing could be done to prevent damage to university buildings.

It is perhaps easy to forget that communication between towns and cities was then by no means as rapid as it is today. Events occurring in Edinburgh might as well have been a world away from those occurring in Aberdeen. In fact, when Edinburgh students were dissecting cadavers and discussing the finer details of the human body, the students in Aberdeen had not seen so much as a dog grace their dissecting table for over two years.

The Aberdeen Medical Society was founded on 22 December 1789 and, as with all new societies, the enthusiasm and determination of the young students was obvious from the outset. Minutes were kept of the evening meetings and a set of 'Regulations of the Medical Society' were drawn up. Papers written by Society members were discussed at meetings and discussions were even carried out regarding the length of time the president should be able to remain in office. Less than three months later, the Society was dissecting a dog and all seemed to be progressing well. That is, however, until 1794 when the availability of both animals and human cadavers dried up completely.

In May of that year, the Society received a letter from its founding members who were now based in London: George Kerr, Alexander Mitchell, Colin Allan, James McGrigor, William Hendrie and George Rose. The letter not only remarked on the good reputation the Society had in London, but also suggested that it should purchase anatomical preparations. The founding members also recommended the study of anatomy.

Disappointed to hear that dissections were being neglected in Aberdeen, the letter aimed to provide a few words of encouragement:

> 'We are certain that proper subjects might easily be had there [Aberdeen], and will certainly be had unless the students are wanting to themselves in spirited exertion or in common prudence. Bodies are procured in London for dissection almost every day; we leave anyone to form an opinion whether it would not be an easier affair at Aberdeen.'

These words of encouragement from one of the Society's founding members were all it seems to have taken for the Aberdeen students to establish a supply of cadavers, which were soon available for future meetings. This is not to say that an abundance of subjects suddenly graced the dissecting tables, but a steady supply of material was promptly at hand. There appears to have been some hesitation, however, for the Society wrote to George Rose, one of the founding members, asking for 'subjects' in March 1797. Rose replied, 'I am persuaded that a subject now and then might be procured at Aberdeen, and much knowledge might be acquired if the inspection of bodies at the Hospital was more attended to.'

By 1800, the Society was becoming more accustomed to procuring corpses by extracting them from the local burial grounds. Two students, a Mr Milne and Mr Nimmo, got into hot water that April when they were implicated with taking up a dead body which had already been dissected from an undisclosed location. Both of the students absented themselves from future meetings to allow the Society to come to some arrangement over a suitable punishment. Mr Milne was allowed to resign, while Mr Nimmo was fined half a guinea, as well as being reprimanded in front of the whole Society.

The stigma and dishonour attached to acquiring subjects for dissection in such an unsavoury manner did not dissuade the Society from forging ahead with its plans. In June 1801, the Society stipulated that every member absenting himself from the taking up or depositing of a dead body which was to be used for dissection was to be fined 10s 6d, unless they had a valid excuse. By the following year a new clause was added to the regulations, stating that 'any member not willing to be present at the taking up of bodies is not obliged to pay the guinea unless he attend the dissection'. The rules were therefore quite clear: if you were not prepared to risk getting caught digging up a corpse, then you would not be permitted to dissect one.

The increasing demand for anatomical teaching in both England and Scotland, combined with the illegality and unsavoury nature of bodysnatching, meant that there was insufficient time for lecturers and students to carry on securing their own material, had they wished to do so.

Perhaps one of the best sources for gauging the number of students studying anatomy in England derives from the 'Report from the Select Committee on Anatomy', compiled to 'inquire into the manner of obtaining Subjects for Dissection in the Schools of Anatomy' in July 1828. The Report suggests that the legal supply of cadavers would have been adequate if teaching methods had remained unchanged. When students were taught using only one, or at most two cadavers per course in the early part of the eighteenth century, it was still possible for them to obtain their own subjects for the dissecting table, carrying out raids in a few local churchyards, as and when subjects were needed.

Yet, by 1828, it was recommended that each student should dissect at least three cadavers during their sixteen-month tuition: two for studying the structure of the body and a third for practising operations. If students were to study continuously in order to obtain a 'complete education', then someone else would have to provide material for the practical anatomy lessons. The demand for cadavers could not be met without either some very dedicated students or professional help.

Cadavers had to be dissected rapidly to make the best use of each subject and before it had chance to start decaying and become unsuitable for dissection. The abdomen and gut would be worked first, as these were the first areas to start decomposing. The methodical dissection of the rest of the body would then follow. In the winter months this meant completing the dissection in ten days, whilst in the summer, this deadline was reduced by half. With dissection playing a large part in medical studies, there was simply not enough time for students to procure their own cadaver and dissect it before the body became unfit for purpose.

When Hunter opened his school in 1746, followed by other new private anatomy schools in the capital, student numbers were at first manageable and the system of students procuring their own cadavers worked well. Numbers increased steadily with about 300 students studying in London alone by 1798. Twenty-five years later, this number had risen by 700 and along with this dramatic rise in student numbers, an equally dramatic demand for cadavers also arose. With an estimated 1000 medical students in London by 1828, it was no longer possible for lecturers and students to provide their own subjects, although some did like to keep their hand in if a particularly interesting subject became available. Not only was there little time for graveyard raids, but the high numbers of cadavers required meant that it was becoming increasingly difficult to keep exhumations out of the public eye.

To meet this demand, students would have had to raid churchyards on a more frequent basis and risk ruining their future careers. The alternative was to pass the whole operation over to professionals who could provide the anatomy schools with a steady supply of fresh cadavers. This shift was at first gradual. Bribing corrupt sextons with a few pence from their allowance, slowly adapted into paying a bodysnatcher to bring a cadaver to the back door of the anatomy school. This, in turn, led to the rise of professional bodysnatching gangs, who mainly operated in larger cities such as London or Liverpool. It also provided an opportunity for men in the provinces to make some extra money, if they were clever enough to realise the potential of this commodity.

Chapter 1

The Beginnings of Bodysnatching in England & Scotland

'Yesterday morning an attempt was made in open day to rob a churchyard in the neighbourhood of London. A wretch . . . seeing a grave dug, and a coffin already in it, broke it open, and took out the bodies (there happening to be more than one) with which he was making off; but being seen . . . he was seized and committed to Bridewell.'
                                       – *Oxford Journal*, Saturday, 31 March 1759.

The discovery of someone stripping grave clothes from a corpse in a churchyard in the middle of the afternoon is naturally suspicious. Yet, one Dublin gravedigger named John Loftus was seen in the Round Church graveyard one afternoon in May 1732 doing just that. Although Loftus's case is often cited when discussing early examples of bodysnatching, instead of stealing the cadaver for use by a surgeon, Loftus was in fact after human fat.

Not all exhumations made it to the dissecting table and John Loftus had realised that the fat produced when boiling a cadaver was a valuable commodity. It later transpired that Loftus had 'plunder[ed] of above fifty [graves], not only for their coffins and burial cloaths (sic), but of their fat, where bodies afforded any, which he retailed at a high price.' While shocking to modern standards, using by-products of cadavers was not unknown during the eighteenth century. It can be surmised from an incriminating line in a poem written in 1796 by Robert Southey, 'The Surgeon's Warning': 'I have made candles of infants' fat.'

Another failed attempt at selling a cadaver to the surgeons occurred in 1802 after a tussle arose at the gallows between a group of surgeons and the friends of a hanged shoemaker, who were trying to claim their friend's body to give him a Christian burial. The friends won and took the body back to his widow's home, naturally expecting thanks for their efforts. Rather uncharitably, the widow had removed herself from the situation, leaving the shoemaker's friends with a body on their hands which they now needed to dispose of. In a complete turn of events, the shoemaker's friends now tried, in vain, to sell his body to the apothecaries situated between Horsley and Rotherhithe, but even at a reduced rate no one was interested. Defeated, they covered the body in pitch and hastily buried it in St George's Fields.

Students and surgeons were yet to fear for their reputations or the risk of being caught by the mob if found violating a grave. They could afford to turn away cadavers that appeared randomly for sale at their back doors. Whilst demand for cadavers remained manageable and the general population was unaware of events taking place in local churchyards, the surgeons and their students did not think twice about entering graveyards at night to ensure there was a body to dissect at the next morning's lecture.

As the century progressed, however, things changed. Students and lecturers began to be prosecuted as local people became more aware that bodies were going missing and, as a result, medical students visited more far-flung churchyards. Pilfering of graves was not restricted to the environs of London or the major Scottish centres for anatomical training either. In 1792 Berwick parish church was the target of a raid by three young surgeons. A local mob tore down the house of one of the perpetrators, 24-year-old surgeon and student of physic Robert Nesbitt, after it was discovered that the trio had been stealing dead bodies from the churchyard and storing them inside Nesbitt's house.

Nesbitt, described in the papers as being 'very deaf' with 'a custom of turning his head to one side when he is spoken to', absconded, and a reward of twenty guineas was offered by the parish vestry to anyone who apprehended him. Nesbitt's accomplices, George Miller and Thomas Yellowly, were not so quick on their feet and both men appeared in court indicted for stealing the body of Christian Ross, the wife of John Ross on 31 July 1792. The young surgeons were also found to be in possession of a child's body, together with his coffin, as well as the body of an unknown female.

The two young surgeons, together with a further accomplice William Burn, all denied their involvement in the exhumation, which subsequently resulted in a verdict of not guilty by the jury. Nesbitt, on the other hand, was never caught and no further record of him involved in this or any subsequent bodysnatching scandal has been found.

Berwickshire would be hit with a further bodysnatching scandal in 1820, this time in Coldingham when a Dr Lowry was convicted of 'lifting up and carrying away' a dead body from the parish churchyard. Suspicion was aroused when a large number of goods were requested to be delivered from his house to Edinburgh 'without delay'. After taking charge of one particular trunk, it soon became apparent that the container was emitting a nauseating smell. Other passengers waiting to travel to Edinburgh insisted that it be investigated immediately. After the lid was forced open, their suspicions were confirmed when out tumbled the body of a grey-haired woman, a former parishioner of Coldingham. The smell of her decomposing corpse had filtered through the trunk, despite her having been embalmed and packed carefully 'amidst a variety of perfumes'. Lowry was sentenced to six months' imprisonment in Greenlaw Gaol and a subsequent six weeks in Canongate Tollbooth, Edinburgh.

It appears that Dr Lowry was in the habit of stealing the bodies of the recently interred from the parish churchyard and storing them at his home. An article in the *Berwickshire News and General Advertiser* published in 1906 stated that Lowry was working hand-in-hand with 'all the body-snatchers in the district'. When a corpse arrived at his house, it would be passed through a small window in the gable end known as 'Resurrection Window'.

Coaches were often used to transport cadavers across the country and in 1797 the December issue of the *Ipswich Journal* included a story about hackney coachman Samuel Taylor. The coachman was arrested on the suspicion that he was working with a bodysnatcher by the name of Hutton. After the parish watch saw Taylor's coach pull up outside the burial ground on Old Street Road, London they wasted no time in challenging him. Taylor was found to have the bodies of a man and three children in his possession. They also discovered that a number of bodies had been hidden under the wall of the churchyard, ready for transportation at a later date. It was believed that all the corpses buried in the churchyard over the five weeks preceding Taylor's capture had been removed from their graves – around fifteen a week.

In order to transport Taylor to the New Prison in Clerkenwell so that he could be brought before the magistrates, he was thrown into the back of his own coach along with the rotting corpses he had stolen. He must have been tired after all his efforts that evening, for it was reported that he fell asleep in the back of the coach, alongside the corpses and the authorities had some difficulty waking him up when they arrived at their destination.

As the need for more cadavers increased, so the methods of procurement began to alter. In London, the Hunter brothers were both involved in obtaining bodies for anatomy lectures by the mid-eighteenth century. William would send his students out to assist grave-robbers and the students themselves would bribe the sextons. It did not usually take much to persuade these poorly paid employees of the church to bend the rules just a little. A few pence was often all that was needed to ensure a little help, just sufficient to make sure that a gate to the churchyard was left open.

The younger of the Hunter brothers, John, became quite adept at exhuming corpses for his brother's lectures, taking with him a number of students to help with the exhumation and to carry the cadavers. By day John worked as a demonstrator in his elder brother's lectures, pointing out the intricate workings of the human body, whilst William explained the structure to the students. By night he would liaise with the most depraved characters of the London streets in order to keep his brother's promise to teach students in the 'Paris Manner', for each student to have a corpse of their own to dissect.

John is perhaps most famed for acquiring the body of Irishman Charles Byrne in 1783. Byrne is stated to have been over 7ft tall and he knew that his body was desired by anatomists. They were eager to investigate why he had grown so tall and, after dissecting his corpse, would have been fascinated to see his skeleton, although they would have struggled to fit his thigh bones and tibia into a pot to boil away the fat. John Hunter successfully obtained Byrne's body, even though Byrne's friends had promised him that he would be safe from the anatomist's table.

Today, Byrne's skeleton is on display at the Hunterian Museum at the Royal College of Surgeons, London, for all to see. Byrne's friends sold his corpse for £500 (the equivalent of over £31,000 today), forgetting their promise to bury his body in a leaden coffin far out at sea. This was a princely sum and they must have reasoned that, after all, Byrne would be none the wiser.

Before 1800, the rising demand for cadavers among anatomists was evident throughout England and many anatomy courses had begun to be advertised by medical schools outside London. In 1777 Bristol Infirmary was providing 'Courses of Anatomy', for which bodies were procured from London, presumably by illicit means. Similarly, in 1776 a Mr Hunt was offering a 'Course in Anatomical and Chirurgical Lectures' at his home in Burford, Oxfordshire, for the price of two guineas, with each course lasting about six weeks. Hunt's advert, which appeared in the *Oxford Journal*, stated that 'there will be one body for dissections and another for operations in every course.' Where did he get his supply of cadavers from, one wonders? Perhaps the charge of 'three Guineas and a half for each body' was enough to pay off the bodysnatcher or sexton and still ensure he was able to pocket a profit.

But not everyone was able to procure bodies so readily, as can be seen from an advert placed by Newcastle surgeon Mr William Smith in the *Newcastle Chronicle* for 'Lectures on Midwifery and Anatomy' commencing in November 1782: 'Mr Smith proposes . . . to instruct . . . in the knowledge of the Human Body from wet and dry preparations of the bones, muscles, blood vessels etc.' No fresh cadavers for his students.

While bodysnatching had evidently spread across the country, most of the earliest recorded cases took place within the capital, rather than the provinces. Often, however, these cases were merely anecdotes reported in newspapers to excite the general public or mere rumours, with few cases casting any real light on who the bodysnatchers were.

In 1765, the *Oxford Journal* included an unusual level of detail within a story involving bodysnatchers William Holt and Abraham Evans. The pair had been tried for stealing the body of a child from the parish churchyard of St Andrews, Holborn. Holt received four months' imprisonment in Newgate Gaol and was ordered to pay a fine of one shilling, whilst Evans received four months in the Compter – probably the Poultry Compter, a sheriffs' prison within the city of London – and was also fined one shilling. In contrast, a more typical report appearing in the *Universal Magazine* in 1796 provides no clues as to who might have targeted a churchyard in Cripplegate and subsequently sold 'divers bodies' to the surgeons for two guineas each.

One of the biggest cases before the turn of the eighteenth century occurred in February 1795 in London, when three men were disturbed whilst trying to remove bodies from Lambeth burial ground. When inquiries were made, it transpired that the three men in question were part of a fifteen–strong gang which included a gravedigger, coachmen and 'eight surgeons of public repute'. The bodies had been procured from about thirty burial grounds in the area and were subsequently sold at a set price: 'for an adult two Guineas and a crown, for every one under age, [children] six shillings, for the first foot and nine-pence per inch'.

Reports stated that some of the bodies, once prepared by the articulator (of human skeletons), were sent to America and the West Indies whilst 'many with the flesh on [were] made into skeletons [and] sent to different parts of this kingdom'. Perhaps most shockingly of all was the end use that some of the snatched corpses were put to. The report claimed that the articulator not only 'substituted human skulls for nail boxes' but also '[gave] the skeleton of a child, instead of a doll, for his own child to play with.'

As reports like these proliferated, the public became increasingly wary of bodysnatchers and began to respond to rumours of their presence, at times violently. This can be seen throughout the history of Scotland when one of the earliest accounts of bodysnatching occurred in 1678. It was rumoured that the body of a 16-year-old gypsy, who had been hanged for murder along with three family members, had been taken from Greyfriars Kirkyard, Edinburgh by surgeons 'to make an anatomical dissection of'. The discovery of the disturbed grave on the morning of 6 February led to a few different conclusions, including the theory that the hanged felon had survived his punishment and risen from the grave.

However, the very first confirmed account of bodysnatching for the purposes of dissection in Scotland occurred once again at Greyfriars, when medical students raided the kirkyard in 1711. The corpse of Robert Findlay was found to have been taken from his grave, with the populace blaming both the surgeons and the gravedigger. As a result, the Incorporation of Surgeons threatened their apprentices with expulsion if they were found violating the graves in an attempt to secure 'subjects' for their medical training.

Fourteen years later, Edinburgh would again be up in arms regarding the conduct of its medical students. A mob threatened to ransack Surgeons' Hall, which housed Alexander Monro's lecture theatre, after students were once again caught violating graves in the city. These threats were enough to send Monro in search of safer lecture rooms within the University buildings.

As far as riots go, the 1742 riot in Edinburgh was quite something. The stealing of the Portsburgh drum – used by the town guard to alert people in the neighbourhood to any disturbances – the destruction of any houses and shops possessing the slightest association with anatomists and the burning down of 'Resurrection Hall' all took place before the authorities could grasp what was happening.

Tensions had run high through the city for a number of months in the spring of that year, coming to a head when the public received word that surgeon Martin Eccles, together with his eager band of apprentices had obtained the body of Alexander Baxter, who had been interred in St Cuthbert's Kirkyard (formerly West Kirk) only one week previously. The kirkyard was such a favoured haunt of the medical fraternity that, in 1738, the height of the boundary wall had been increased to 8ft in an effort to stop the raids. Needless to say, these efforts were fruitless.

The first night of riots in the city occurred on 9 March, when an angry mob gathered outside the premises of surgeon Martin Eccles, after the body of the recently buried Alexander Baxter had been found on his premises. Windows were smashed and doors broken down, as the mob shouted abuse to Eccles and the surgeons of Edinburgh, leaving them in no doubt as to how they felt about the theft of their loved ones' bodies.

Gaining support as the night wore on, the mob seized the Portburgh Drum and proceeded to beat to arms along the Cowgate to Niddery's Wynd. Here the mob was confronted by the City Guard and stopped before they could incite any more anger. The mob did not need a drum to show its disgust towards Eccles and the other surgeons of the city. Windows of homes belonging to surgeons were smashed, whether or not they had played any part in stealing the body of Alexander Baxter. As far as the mob was concerned, all surgeons were the same; they all had little regard for the sanctity of the grave and the corpse within it.

Still angered by the previous night's discovery, the mob rose again the following evening, this time entering Eccles's shop and destroying it completely. Magistrates, the City Guard and High Constables were rallied to help disperse the mob, many of whom escaped through the Netherbow Port. With the city gates locked up and the mob trapped on the wrong side of the city walls, the irate citizens eventually returned home.

Meanwhile, Eccles and his apprentices were charged with removing the dead bodies from their graves. Without warning, two of the apprentices absconded, leaving Eccles and his three remaining apprentices to face the magistrates. Surprisingly, no proof was found to implicate the men and the charges were subsequently dropped.

The mob, however, was not satisfied by the verdict and another rumour began making its way through the city, that George Haldane, a beadle from West Kirk, had been an accessory to the theft of bodies from the kirkyard. The mob descended upon his home, now dubbed 'Resurrection Hall' as it was believed to have been built from the proceeds of bodysnatching. There they found fragments of old coffins, which incited them further. The next day the mob went back to finish what they had started and set fire to the property, destroying it completely.

On 18 March, three days after his house has been destroyed, Haldane inserted a public notice in the newspapers, declaring his innocence:

> 'All Doctors and Surgeons in Edinburgh or about it, or within the
> Kingdom of Scotland, or any other person that can make it evident that
> I had any hand or part in lifting the corpse in the West church yard, I
> come in the judges' hands to suffer death.'

By this time, the Edinburgh mob had dispersed into the surrounding neighbourhoods and on the same day Haldane declared his innocence, another mob was targeting the house of Peter Richardson. Yet another man suspected of bodysnatching for the surgeons, Richardson was a gardener living at Inveresk, five miles from Edinburgh.

Public discontent with the situation rumbled on throughout the rest of March, with incidents continually being recorded throughout the city. Finally, on 6 April 1742 things came to a head when the guards who controlled the city gates stopped

John Samuel at the Potterrow Port. The parcel he had been carrying was found to contain the dead body of Gaston Johnston, the recently deceased child of Robert Johnston, who had only just been buried in Pentland Kirkyard, six miles away from Edinburgh.

Samuel had been caught up in the riots the month before, when the mob had threatened to destroy his home, suspecting his involvement in bodysnatching. But, after much persuasion from his neighbours, Samuel's home had been saved on the understanding that he distanced himself from such practices in the future.

This time Samuel would not be as fortunate. Upon his release by the authorities, the mob heard the tale of his attempt to sell little Gaston Johnston's body and once again visited Samuel's home at Grangegateside. Samuel's house was destroyed, but he had already absconded. He was arrested later the next day and brought to trial at the Court of Justiciary in July. Although found not guilty of opening Gaston's grave, Samuel was convicted of being in possession of a dead child. With the guilty verdict delivered, all that remained was to pass sentence. Unlike the surgeons, Samuel did not get off lightly: he was sentenced to be whipped through the streets of Edinburgh and subsequently banished from Scotland for seven years.

Disgust towards the violation of graves by medical students spread throughout Scotland, beyond the major cities. In 1724 students were caught raising bodies from Greyfriars burial ground in Perth. In response the Town Council offered a ten pound reward to anyone who could provide information on the event and threatened that surgeons found to be involved in bodysnatching would receive not only a twenty-pound fine but also lose their practice. Apprentices involved were also to be fined a sum of five pounds, as well as being 'whipped and pilloried'.

A year later, Kelso was to be the centre of a bodysnatching attempt, when three local men came under the scrutiny of the law. John Gibson, doctor of medicine, together with Alexander Herriot and William Pringle – the latter the son of a surgeon and the former a servant to William Pringle's father – were tried on suspicion of having stolen the body of Richard Aitchison. Evidence given at the trial in May 1725 by William Ramsey, the son of the Kelso minister James Ramsey, suggested that the accused had been either involved or suspected of disinterring the dead for the purposes of dissection before.

As events unfolded in the Justiciary Court at Jedburgh, it became apparent that Richard Aitchison was not the only body that the trio had exhumed. Ramsey recounted that the body of an Andrew Gramslaw had been taken from his grave in Kelso churchyard the previous November. He also stated that he had received a visit from John Foreman, a servant to Dr Gibson, who had taken him to a loft belonging to the doctor and showed him the body of a child lying on a table.

The child was proven to be Walter, the son of Kelso cordwainer Robert Dalgleish.

Ramsey stated that he had seen all of the accused standing in the loft above Gibson's stables that night, including the doctor's own son, Thomas. He even went so far as to say he had seen Alexander Herriot, servant to the Kelso surgeon James Pringle, (father of the accused William Pringle) with a scalpel in his hand, removing Walter's skin in order to examine his muscles. However, when Ramsey was questioned about the disappearance of Richard Aitchison, he could provide no further evidence, other than to confirm the suspicions of the people of Kelso.

Further evidence from local men revealed that, after rumours of bodysnatching surfaced, a number of women had gone to Kelso churchyard to dig up the coffin of Robert Aitchison. When the lid was removed, the coffin was found to be empty. The women then marched to Dr Gibson's stables, where they discovered Robert's body on the table, still clad in his grave clothes. Despite everything, the case appears to have fallen apart and no further evidence was presented. Dr Gibson's son Thomas failed to appear in court when summoned as a witness and was subsequently outlawed. Even though they had been presented with evidence that the body had been removed from the grave with its grave clothes, a factor that should have escalated the case to a felony, the jury found the charge not proven.

By the end of the eighteenth century, it was widely known that medical students and lecturers were involved in stealing cadavers on a regular basis. The authorities failed to respond to the violation of city and rural graveyards and friends and relatives of the deceased were being forced to take their own precautions to ensure that when a loved one was interred, their grave really would be their final resting place.

Preventative measures carried out in Scotland would be considerably different to those carried out in England, but the bodysnatchers' methods varied little. Techniques of exhumation and transportation filtered through the macabre underworld, so as to ensure a plentiful supply of cadavers. Prices would fluctuate according to levels of supply and demand, but the threat of the bodysnatcher was only just beginning.

By the turn of the century, demand for bodies among English students and their lecturers' corresponding need to keep a low profile was becoming ever more heightened. London would see the rise of the influential Borough gang also known as the Crouch gang, whose determination to be the sole supplier of cadavers to the city's medical schools would lead to the great 'cutting scandal' in 1816. Resurrectionists would operate out of different ports and parishes across England and Scotland and discoveries of bodies in pickling barrels, hampers and trunks would, before long, become commonplace.

Chapter 2

First Forays

From student outings to the rise of the professional bodysnatcher

'. . . it must be remembered that many of those implicated were actuated by a sincere desire to further the interests of their profession, and faced obloquy and danger with a great deal of pluck and fortitude.'
– *A History of Bristol Royal Infirmary*, Richard Smith Jnr, (1917).

One September evening in 1825, liquid slowly began oozing across the floor of the coach office of the Turf Hotel in Newcastle. It was coming from a trunk waiting to be delivered to James Syme Esq., of 6 Forth Street, Edinburgh.

The trunk had been left in the wrong office and the subsequent delay had resulted in the leaking fluid escaping its confines and omitting a 'nauseous smell'. On investigation, the trunk was found to contain the body of 'a young woman, about 19 years of age, of fair complexion, light eyes, and yellow hair, and without any marks of violence.'

How had bodysnatching developed from students and lecturers exhuming cadavers to meet their specific needs, to bodies being wedged into trunks and transported on the nation's highways? The act of removing a corpse from the grave had moved on from removing the coffin in order to extract the corpse. By the time the professionals came to dominate the scene in the early nineteenth century, a cadaver could be exhumed and concealed in the waiting sack in less than an hour, with minimal disruption to the grave.

Once a body was exhumed, a variety of different shipment methods would be implemented, usually involving very simple ideas. Large numbers of cold, ashen corpses would pass through ports, coach offices and turnpikes jammed into casks, boxes and barrels, disguised as 'produce' or labelled 'Glass: Handle with Care'.

Before the rise of the professional bodysnatcher in the early 1800s, the only way of obtaining a corpse was by rolling up your sleeves and getting one yourself. Bribing sextons would gain you access to the churchyard, but chances were that you would still have to get your hands dirty to gain a cadaver. The 'mail order' system enabling access to bodies from the far reaches of England and Ireland had yet to develop.

Digging up a cadaver, fresh or otherwise, took a certain amount of skill, which was something that the early bodysnatchers – the students and lecturers – did not always possess. Sensitivity was not their strong point, their main aim was simple: to secure a corpse ready for their next anatomy lecture. Rarely did they consider the effect that violating a grave would have on the local community or indeed the relatives of the deceased. Students opened graves and smashed up coffins, leaving splintered lids and burial clothes strewn across the churchyard waiting to be discovered the next day. Such time and effort was taken by the students to exhume the whole of the coffin that by the time the cadaver had been extracted, they had little consideration for the state of the graveyard.

At this point, ensuring there was a fresh cadaver ready for the next anatomy lesson was the responsibility of a number of individuals, mainly the lecturer, demonstrator or student. In Scotland both the lecturer and his student ventured into the unsavoury practice of bodysnatching, whilst south of the border just having an interest in anatomy seemed to be sufficient reason to participate in an exhumation.

However, soon high demand and the introduction of the 'Paris Manner' by surgeons such as William Hunter, forced medical practitioners to pay professionals to supply them with cadavers. If this method of teaching was to be successfully introduced in Britain, then anatomists were going to need a lot more corpses than the gallows could deliver. William Hunter employed the help of both students and professional resurrection men, almost guaranteeing a continuous supply of cadavers.

Even at the height of his career in the 1820s, Sir Astley Cooper, the eminent surgeon to King George IV, worked so closely with the resurrection men that he would pay maintenance to their families if any of them received a prison sentence whilst snatching corpses for him.

With the meagre supply of six cadavers from the gallows at Tyburn still the only legal means of obtaining a corpse for dissection, English surgeons began to devise ways of accessing corpses. The legal supply was destined for the London College of Surgeons, not the private anatomy schools which had sprung up unchecked within the city. William Hunter would certainly not have been allocated anything.

Some surgeons, like John Hunter, William's brother, were said to visit the gallows on hanging days. Swinging on the legs of a hanging victim hastened their death. But often the men pulling and tugging on the legs of a hanged felon were doing so for very different reasons. 'Tyburn tussles' were increasing, as medical men became desperate enough for subjects to bargain or even fight with the hanged felons' relatives over their corpses.

Until hangings moved inside the walls of Newgate Gaol in 1783, they were the cause of great public entertainment. Tickets would be sold for the best seats at the windows of the surrounding houses and the condemned prisoner would be transported through the streets on the back of a cart. Depending on their crime, the prisoner might be cheered along the route, which more often than not involved a number of stops at taverns along the way. By the time the condemned prisoner reached the foot of the gallows, medical men hoping to be in with a chance of getting the corpse would already be in place, even pretending to be relatives or friends of the convict in the hope of not drawing too much attention to themselves.

In 1765 the *Bath Chronicle* reported a 'great contest at Tyburn . . . between a surgeon mob and the populace . . . the latter however brought off in triumph and delivered [him] to his friends for burial.' Similar rescue attempts were not so successful. In 1768, Daniel Afgood was sentenced to death after murdering a watchman from Blackfriars, London. After his body had been removed from the gallows it was destined for the dissection table at Surgeons' Hall and conveyed to premises on the King's Road in preparation for the journey.

The *Derby Mercury* described how 'about 300 bargemen and lighter-men' made their way to King's Road, in an attempt to rescue Daniel's corpse from the surgeons. A tip-off given to the sheriff alerted the authorities to the rescue attempt and the party was foiled when Daniel's body was 'conveyed another way to the said Hall'.

Bodies were not just seized from the gallows, though. In 1750, Bristol surgeon Abraham Ludlow, with the help of his son (also Abraham) and apothecary John Page, claimed the corpse of 'Long Jack', a recently deceased vagabond of the town. Having committed suicide 'Long Jack' was therefore not entitled to a Christian burial and instead he was to be buried at a crossroads on the edge of town. Stealing out in the dead of night, Ludlow and his associates secured the corpse and wrapping it in a cloth, placed it on the back of a cart and headed for home. Unfortunately, the party found the gates to the city locked, forcing them to rethink their route. They decided to use the pedestrian access to the side of the main gate, and gingerly made their way through the narrow passage.

Perhaps the trio should have considered the nickname of their quarry a little more before making the detour, for Long Jack's corpse was too big to pass through the gates. Before they reached the other side Jack's body fell to the floor with a dull thud. Panicking, the bodysnatchers tried to convince the porter who had rushed out in response to the thud that all was well. With the porter's suspicions quelled by a suitable bribe, Ludlow and colleagues made their way home, placing Jack's corpse on the dissecting table before retiring to bed.

However, when morning arrived a loud cry from the maid alerted Ludlow to the fact that he had forgotten to lock the door to the dissecting room. Not wanting to be caught with a recently exhumed corpse on their hands, the men returned to the crossroads that very night, reburying Long Jack where they had found him.

As the anatomists went to greater lengths to obtain corpses for dissection, friends and relatives of deceased felons began to make additional efforts to ensure that their bodies would be safe from the bodysnatchers once they were buried. Even if friends had succeeded in taking the corpse away from the gallows surgeons would still attempt to steal it. They would simply arrange for someone to grab the corpse from its grave.

Lime or pitch was often sprinkled in to the coffin just before the lid was screwed down, to hasten decomposition. This was the case in 1764, after John Henry Hairman was executed for carrying out a robbery near Lincoln's Inn Fields. His friends had paid an undertaker to bring a hearse to the gallows, so that he might be decently buried. However, Hairman had been a soldier in the First Regiment of Foot Guards and a number of soldiers seized Hairman's corpse as soon as it had been put into his coffin, declaring that no surgeon should have the body of their friend for the dissecting table. They buried Hairman in Tothill Fields, but not before they had covered his coffin in unslaked lime.

Corpses did not just end up on the dissecting table. Surgeons were also keen to acquire specimens for their ever-growing anatomical collections, and competed to get hold of the bodies of men and women who had died of rare diseases. This desire drove many surgeons to offer large amounts of money in an attempt to become the proud owner of an unusual specimen.

As previously mentioned, John Hunter went to great lengths to obtain the body of the Irish Giant Charles Byrne. Similarly, in 1798 when long-serving clerk to the Bank of England William Daniel Jenkins died after a slow decline, his body, which measured over 6ft in height, would have been of most interest to the London surgeons. Excavations carried out in 1933 in the Garden Court, once the churchyard of St Christopher-le-Stocks, unearthed a lead coffin buried 40ft deep and measuring 7ft 6 inches in length. A plate on the coffin lid read 'Mr William Danl. Jenkins. Died 24 March 1798, Aged 31'. Due to his height, Jenkins's friends had feared that the bodysnatchers would try to take him and so they had taken precautions, having already been offered 'upwards of 200 guineas by some surgeons' (equivalent to about £11,000 today).

Not all anatomists were prepared to wait for long-suffering parishioners to die of a mysterious affliction, nor could they pursue the corpse of every man or woman dangling at the gallows. An alternative source of cadavers had to be sought. Students and lecturers therefore ventured out into graveyards on a frequent basis, either raiding those in the immediate vicinity or, as was the case with Robert Nesbitt and his fellow students in 1792, targeting quieter neighbouring villages or those located in the border parishes of England and Scotland.

When the opportunity arose to obtain a fresh cadaver a bodysnatcher had to take it, no matter what the date was. Christmas Day was perhaps not the most pleasant occasion upon which to announce that the churchyard had been targeted by resurrection men but that is what the minister of St Fittick's Church in Aberdeenshire did when he discovered that bodysnatchers had raided his quiet village churchyard in 1808. Strewn across the grass were 'broken pieces of the lid of the coffin, tatters of grave linen, and marks of blood left by the grave'. The corpse taken was that of Mrs Janet Spark, an elderly parishioner who had been buried on 22 December and snatched later the same day. Her body seemed to have disappeared altogether and, fearing the worst, the parishioners knew that there was little they could do about it.

Two months later, her putrid corpse was found on the south side of Nigg Bay. Fearing detection, the bodysnatchers had hastily reburied Janet Spark in the sand near the church on the north side of the bay, planning to dig her up later when the excitement had died down. The British weather had saved Mrs Spark from the anatomist's slab, for a storm blew in preventing the bodysnatchers from returning. The pounding of the waves slowly washed the sand away from around Janet's body, which eventually came free, only to ride the waves and come to a rest on the river bank opposite the church.

Determined students, as well as a very determined young surgeon, were also at the centre of a bodysnatching scandal that caused fury in the city of Glasgow in 1813. The citizens were so enraged that when the time came for the case to be tried, the surgeon involved requested that the trial be heard in Edinburgh, as he feared it would be difficult to find an impartial jury in Glasgow to pass verdict.

The Ramshorn scandal occurred in December 1813 and it involved the anatomist Granville Sharp Pattison. Situated near the medical school on College Street, Glasgow, was the Ramshorn Kirkyard. It was a popular place for the rich of Glasgow to be buried and on 13 December 1813, Mrs Janet McAllaster was duly placed into her grave, the burial solemnly observed by her friends and family. The following morning it was discovered that her grave had been tampered with and a set of footprints left in the morning frost pointed in the direction of College Street.

Word soon spread about the bodysnatching, not only through the populace but also through the medical profession. It was believed by some that Pattison had taken the body of Mrs McAllaster and it was thought that if Pattison could be warned of the discovery, he would endeavour to return the body to the grave 'privately and quietly'. An apprentice was sent to forewarn Pattison of the dangers that lay ahead but unfortunately for Pattison, two churchyards had been targeted by bodysnatchers that night and the apprentice sent word about the wrong raid. Believing that the mob was angry about a snatching at Glasgow Cathedral rather than at Ramshorn Kirkyard, Pattison thought that he was in the clear. He could not have been more wrong.

When the search group, consisting of dentist James Alexander and the senior town officer James Pirrie arrived at Pattison's dissecting rooms, it would take them over half an hour of violent knocking before the door was opened and a search of the premises could be made. They came face-to-face with a number of partially dissected corpses, including 'the body of a woman with her throat laid open', pans of bones boiling in 'blood coloured water' over the fire and 'other pans containing entrails, a heart, a liver, kidneys and lungs'. Dugald McGregor, Janet McAllaster's brother, finally found his sister, or more specifically her head, at the bottom of a tub of water, nestling with two others. The head was missing its lower jaw, nose, upper lip, right ear, both eyes and a few teeth, but Dugald could still recognise his sister's features.

At this point the dentist, James Alexander, having inadvertently just stepped on an ear lying on the dissecting room floor, confirmed without doubt that the teeth belonged to Mrs McAllaster, his former patient. Other parts of Janet's body were found in various pieces throughout the dissecting room and were collected up, so that she could be duly 'put together' like a human jigsaw. Her 'body' was then placed in a new coffin and reburied.

When Pattison was arrested along with the students involved, Robert Monro and John McLean, and fellow surgeon Andrew Russel, the mob that had crowded round the dissecting rooms inevitably turned violent, assaulting the bodysnatchers with mud and stones.

During Pattison's trial, James Alexander elaborated further on the teeth found in the dissecting room, using a mould he had made for Mrs McAllaster's dentures to identify not only her head, but also a jawbone found in the pocket of Robert Monro. After a trial lasting over sixteen hours, Pattison and his colleagues were finally sentenced. Evidence given by 'a number of the most eminent medical men in Glasgow' questioned whether the body that had been reinterred as Janet McAllaster was the same as the body that had been taken. Mrs McAllaster was the mother of eight children and the body pieced together in Pattison's dissecting rooms was that of a virgin.

This uncertainty surrounding the identity of the cadaver would be the saving grace for the four men involved. After what must have seemed like an eternity, the following verdict was presented by the jury foreman:

> 'We all in one voice find the said Andrew Russel and the said John McLean *not guilty*, and find the libel *not proven* against the other two panels Granville Sharp Pattison and Robert Monro.'

A stern warning from Lord Justice followed:

> 'You are now acquitted of the verdict of a respectable jury, and from the present trial I trust you will learn caution and circumspection in your future conduct. You will not consider yourself entitled to violate the graves of the dead, even for the purposes of science.'

Times were changing. Medical student numbers were rising both in Scotland and England; the number in London alone had increased fivefold between 1800 and 1828, with up to 500 students from the Schools of Anatomy in London clamouring to dissect the legal supply of cadavers. By 1826 there were a total of twelve different establishments within London offering anatomy tuition, the majority of these being private anatomy schools. Glasgow student numbers were also on the increase, rising from just 54 in 1790 to 232 in 1810.

It was becoming more obvious that lecturers could not meet the requirements of their students and they slowly started taking a back seat in procuring cadavers, letting either their eager new students or professional bodysnatchers take their place. The populace was also growing increasingly hostile towards the medical community, as it became widely known that surgeons were involved in the macabre practice. If implicated in bodysnatching, the career of even the most promising young doctor could be ruined. Even so, students started to involve themselves more and more in exhumations of the dead. Not only did their involvement help to ensure that there would be a fresh subject for the anatomy lesson, but some students, especially in Glasgow, found that acquiring cadavers helped to fund their studies.

Yet, as time went on, students preferred to pay someone else rather than involve themselves personally in bodysnatching. The medical students roaming the streets of Georgian Britain often endeavoured to get willing sextons on board with their plans; however, they didn't always find help available.

Students of Bristol Infirmary found that a complaint had been lodged against them in 1769. In fact, the whole of the student body had earned the complaint, after it was discovered that a corpse had been removed from a coffin and substituted for 'a quantity of sand and wool'. Investigations narrowed down the culprits to just a few individuals, who were given a week to think over their actions. Although notes kept by Richard Smith, surgeon to Bristol Infirmary 1796-1843, do not show what happened, we can surmise the final outcome, for 'the key of the dead-house be always in the custody of the Apothecary'. The Bristol medical fraternity was once again in trouble in 1806, when it was discovered that nurses from St Peter's Hospital had been leaving coffins open, allowing the surgeons from the Infirmary to access the dead bodies of paupers.

Scotland's students were equally as embroiled in the macabre practice. In 1817, a case was heard in Aberdeen concerning three students, James Taylor, John Gordon and George Pirie, who were apprenticed to John Gordon, a surgeon in Keith, Moray. They were accused of stealing the recently interred body of John Bremner. The three apprentices all pleaded guilty, yet due to their age and 'other circumstances' it was recommended that they be given clemency. However, after weighing up all the facts, including the defendants' promise to pay compensation to the relatives of the deceased and 'their ingenuous confession of the offence', the young gentlemen each received four months' imprisonment in Banff Gaol.

Edinburgh student Robert Liston was keen to practice his operating skills before entering the medical profession. He believed the best way to do that was to work with professional London bodysnatcher Ben Crouch, who offered to teach him how best to procure a body. The pair stole cadavers from the coastal parish of Rosyth, Fife, located on the banks of the Forth. On one occasion, they left their Edinburgh base and rowed over the waters of the Forth to secure the body of a deceased sailor. Waiting until the sailor's sweetheart had finished grieving by his graveside, Liston and Crouch wasted no time in securing the corpse when the coast was clear. Stuffing the body into a sack, they made a hasty retreat across the water.

In another coastal raid they dressed up as sailors and exhumed a corpse from Culross Churchyard in Fife. Securing the corpse of a deceased female in a sack, they concealed the body under a hedge whilst they took a little light refreshment at the local inn. When the pair were halfway through their drinks, the door of the inn burst open and the barmaid's brother appeared in the doorway. Not only was he delighted to have returned from his travels but he had also happened upon a sack under a hedge on his way in and was curious to know what it might contain. 'If it ain't something good, rot them chaps there who stole it,' exclaimed the sailor, or so the story goes, as he pointed at Liston and Crouch. When the naked body of the female fell out of the sack the shock was enough to render the poor sailor temporarily motionless, giving Liston enough time to snatch the body before the pair made a run for it.

Liston later became a prominent surgeon, reportedly so skilled in amputations that it is said he could remove a limb in twenty-eight seconds. On one occasion, he carried out an amputation so quickly he failed to notice that, with a swift flick of the knife, he had also removed two of his assistant's fingers and the patient's left testicle.

Many students carried on bodysnatching without the assistance of their lecturers. In 1813, three Aberdeen students were caught stealing a cadaver from the churchyard in Banchory-Devenick. Each was fined twenty pounds, the proceeds being given to the poor of the parish. The same year saw Glasgow students having to face the consequences after their habit of raiding the inner city churchyards was discovered. The University issued a new rule: if any student was linked with bodysnatching they would be expelled. The thrill of acquiring a fresh cadaver for the dissecting room table was not going to abate with the threat of expulsion. Even so, by the time professional bodysnatchers were beginning to emerge, student involvement in the midnight raids had thinned out considerably.

The promise of an extra few shillings or even a gold sovereign in the palm of your hand was often more than tempting for a working man, especially if he was trying to support his family in the harsh conditions of Georgian Britain. A few bribes of a shilling here and a few pence there was sometimes all that was needed for the watch to turn a blind eye or even to assist the bodysnatchers in gaining access to the churchyard.

The men who became bodysnatchers were usually down on their luck individuals, who often had links with churchyards or the medical establishments, like hospital porters or gravediggers. Men with honest trades could still find themselves working as bodysnatchers, either independently or with a gang

The professional bodysnatcher did not just burst on to the scene overnight, causing the medical students and lecturers to breathe a sigh of relief that their snatching days were behind them. These men noticed a gap in the market and decided to act upon it. In London, unscrupulous men like Ben Crouch, Patrick Murphy and Joseph Naples, members of the notorious Borough Gang, took on the task of wholesale bodysnatching and made a good job of it.

Members of the Borough Gang came from various sectors of society. Joseph Naples was a former gravedigger, as was Bill Hollis, both men having fallen into the pay of the gang after trying to supply the hospitals on a private basis. Other gang members, like Daniel Butler and Tom Light, ended up in Crouch's gang after a period of bad fortune. At the peak of their success, the gang consisted of between six and seven members and had a number of different leaders, the most influential being Ben Crouch. A sharp-dressing prize fighter, Crouch would refuse to let individual bodysnatchers operate on what he termed his patch and liked to make it known that he was the main, if not the sole supplier of cadavers to St Bartholomew's Hospital and the United Borough Hospitals (now St Thomas' and Guy's).

A professional gang needed a set of rules and these were formulated for every stage in the bodysnatching operation – from delivery to finishing money. The price of a cadaver was agreed upon with the buyer prior to delivery. Resurrection men and surgeons alike referred to corpses as 'subjects' or 'things', whether male or female, young or old. Corpses were priced on a sliding scale, depending on their age and size. An adult of either sex, generally over three feet in length, would sell for about £4 4s in around 1810. A 'small', 'large small', or 'foetus', was a body measuring three feet or less and was priced by the inch.

Professional bodysnatchers were known by a variety of different names during their heyday: 'sack 'em up men', resurrectionists, 'shushy lifters' or 'stealers of the dead'. Whatever they were called, they invariably requested payment up front from the surgeons before, after and during the 'season'. The season ran from October to May and covered the period during which anatomy was taught, both in private anatomy schools and in the teaching hospitals. A corpse gave off a strong enough odour without the added problem of heat, therefore dissection usually took place only during the cooler seasons.

Retainers were a large part of the agreement between the surgeon and the bodysnatcher, with both 'opening' and 'finishing money' being paid at the start and end of each term. Opening money was theoretically used to bribe sextons and watchmen, so that it would be easier for the resurrectionists to gain access to the grave. In reality, this money was more often pocketed.

Not only did the anatomists have to contend with keeping the bodysnatchers happy, they also had to make sure they were looked after when the schools were closed and also when things did not go quite to plan. At the end of the season, consideration had to be made as to how the resurrectionist would live through the summer months without a steady wage. The profits made from bodysnatching were rarely saved and so they requested 'finishing money' to tide them over. In 1827, Sir Astley Cooper noted that he paid six pounds six shillings finishing money to three members of the Borough Gang, and he paid the same sum again two years later. By paying out finishing money surgeons could guarantee a fresh supply of cadavers when the season started up again.

If their regular bodysnatcher was sent to prison or fined whilst securing a cadaver, then any costs incurred fell to the surgeon in question. The anatomist was expected to pay for the keep of the bodysnatcher's family whilst he was locked up, including their lodgings, food and any simple everyday expenses that could no longer be met whilst the family breadwinner was imprisoned.

Records of such payments can be found amongst the papers of Sir Astley Cooper and have been quoted in relation to this topic on many an occasion:

'January 29th 1828, paid Mr. Cock to pay Mr South half the expenses of bailing [Thomas] Vaughan from Yarmouth and going down £14 7s 0d 1829, May 6th, Paid Vaughan's wife 6s. Paid Vaughan for twenty-six weeks confinement at 10s per week, £13 0s 0d.'

Nevertheless, the bodysnatcher's release from prison meant even more expense for the surgeon, who would then have been expected to pay another sum in the form of compensation, to allay the 'inconvenience' of being arrested.

In some cases, such arrangements could get out of hand. When anatomist Joshua Brookes of Blenheim Street School, London refused to pay up front for a cadaver, he learnt that disputing the demands of the bodysnatchers could have consequences. The fee requested by the bodysnatchers was five pounds, which Brookes refused to pay. During the night two badly decomposed bodies were left at either end of Blenheim Street. The bodies were discovered by two women early the next morning and the crowd that quickly gathered outside Brookes's school needed to be controlled by police to prevent Brookes from being injured.

In an attempt to control the ever-increasing demands of the bodysnatchers, lecturers banded together to share their experiences. The Anatomical Club held regular meetings at the Freemasons' Tavern in Great Queen Street, London. Membership was restricted to the lecturers of the teaching hospitals, leaving the teachers from the private schools to fend for themselves. The aim of the Club was to find a solution to the unfortunate position they found themselves in and to stem the extortionate demands of Crouch and his gang. As one member John Flint South noted, 'the resurrection men had . . . always endeavour[ed] to screw more money out of the teachers, either as a bonus, or by striving to obtain a larger price for subjects.'

Yet, an attempt to try to outwit Crouch and foil his outrageous demands backfired. When the bodysnatchers' prices started to creep up surgeons refused to pay, but as a result they found it increasingly difficult to secure cadavers. As Crouch and his gang had such a monopoly, there were few alternative resurrection men to turn to for supplies. In retaliation the bodysnatchers had gone on strike.

In 1811, the *Morning Post* included a small article on 28 October, stating:

'Last winter they [bodysnatchers] entered into a similar conspiracy and their Anatomical friends acceded to the proposed advance of a guinea a body. At that time they received three guineas a corpse, and they now demand five guinea's per body, male and female. The surgeons have in vain remonstrated with them.'

Two days later, newspapers were reporting that an agreement had been reached between the bodysnatchers and the anatomists. The *Morning Chronicle* confirmed that the two sides 'mean to *bury* their animosities in oblivion . . . agreeing to a rise of one guinea per subject.'

An apparent justification for the price rise, following a general complaint made by the surgeons of London, had appeared nearly a year previously in *Jackson's Oxford Journal:*

> 'they [bodysnatchers] expend a large portion of their profit in bribing watchmen to sleep while they are employed in the burying grounds; sextons for leaving the churchyard gates unlocked; hackney coachmen for carrying off their goods . . . [and] the increased price for every necessary of life.'

The 1811 strike lasted for four weeks, with the resurrection men entering the graveyards once again on the night of 28 November.

Ben Crouch was equally ruthless towards would-be bodysnatchers. Any anatomist who thought that they could perhaps outwit their regular resurrectionist and get a corpse cheaper elsewhere, had to think again. Any individual who thought they could do a better job supplying the anatomists was targeted and forced out of business. Graveyards were set upon and spoiled. Putrefied corpses were dug from their graves and strewn across the churchyard, ensuring the parishioners found them the next morning and, if the sexton had been supplying the anatomists (as was the case with gang member Joseph Naples), they would be forced to join Crouch's gang.

However, the current state of affairs could not run smoothly forever. The 'great cutting scandal' of 1816 arose due to the gang's requests for more money. The Anatomical Club refused the demands of the new leader of the gang, Patrick Murphy. He wanted an additional two guineas a body, which would bring the asking price for a 'large' to six guineas a piece, the equivalent of nearly a year's wage for a craftsman.

The price of a single adult corpse would gradually rise to sixteen guineas, before the news of the Burke and Hare case broke in Edinburgh to an astonished public. Yet, in 1816, committing murder on a large scale to supply the anatomy schools had not yet been experimented with. The price demanded by Murphy left the anatomists looking around for an alternative supplier.

The *Stamford Mercury* called the event 'a strange piece of work'; that someone else could possibly supply cadavers to the needy surgeons was an idea no one in the Borough Gang could contemplate. Meanwhile, the surgeons in want of subjects recognised that other men were just as willing to supply cadavers as the Borough Gang and at a cheaper rate.

This situation caused turmoil. Members of the gang 'grossly misconducted themselves' by entering the dissecting room at St Thomas' Hospital, where they assaulted two students, and then proceeding to cut and destroy three cadavers lying on the dissecting tables ready for lectures the following morning. Feelings were clearly running high, for the bodysnatchers visited the dissecting rooms again a few days later and destroyed the bodies of more subjects, rendering them useless.

The surgeons now had three choices: purchase new cadavers, cancel the lecture or comply with Murphy's demands. Murphy won the day and the gang's regular supply of cadavers started trickling into the anatomy schools of London once again.

The success of the Borough Gang cannot be discussed without the mention of an astonishing document, which is preserved by the Royal College of Surgeons in London. The document is a diary, of which only sixteen pages have survived. It precisely charts the dealings of the gang during the period of 28 November 1811 to 5 December 1812. The diary has been attributed to the bodysnatcher Joseph Naples, who sat down each morning and recorded the number of cadavers lifted, the prices received and where they were delivered.

Although incomplete, this 'Diary of a Resurrectionist' provides some of the greatest detail relating to this macabre practice. It also shows the rivalries at work within the Borough Gang and highlights the bickering and corrupt nature of a group of grown men who had set their sights on making an easy profit. Ben Crouch, as the head of the gang, received all the payments for the cadavers, with the other gang members having little or no trust in their leader when it came to sharing out the profits.

The diary provides some colourful accounts of the lives of the gang members: 'Tuesday 10 December 1811: Intoxsicated [sic] all day: at night went out got 5 [bodies] Bunhill Row. Jack [Harnett] all most buried.' The unfortunate Harnett being intoxicated at the time, had slipped on the edge of a grave and tumbled in, taking armfuls of loose soil with him. He was eventually pulled out by other gang members but experienced severe shock as a result of nearly being buried alive.

Two days later, Bunhill Row was their target again: 'went to Bunhill row got 6 [bodies], 1 of them . . . named Mary Rolph, aged 46, Died 5th Dec. 1811.'

The diary also shows the extent of the places to which the gang sent bodies outside London:

> 'Wednesday 15 January 1812: Went to St Thomas's [Hospital], came back, pack'd up 2 large 1 small for Edinburgh.' Saturday 22 February: Met at Barthol[omew's] [Hospital]. Sent 7 to the country, distributed the rest about town [London].'

The success of the Crouch gang is evident not only throughout the pages of the diary, it is also confirmed by the prices paid for subjects in Sir Astley Cooper's own records. Referring to gang member Patrick Murphy, Cooper recalled 'on one occasion [Murphy] was paid £72 for six subjects'. Although this money was used to pay the 'underlings in his employ', Cooper also records that '[on] the same evening at another school he received £72 for another six subjects'. Not bad for one night's work.

Money was clearly the driving factor for the gang, for on 18 March 1812 Naples writes 'at home all night which was a very bad thing for us as we wanted some money to pay our debts to several persons who were importunate.' By 5 April this was all settled: 'Met [the gang] and settled £108 13s. 7d. each man's share £18 2s. 3d.'

The attention brought about by the 'cutting scandal' and the over exaggerated demands of Crouch and Murphy, as well as inter-gang rivalries, meant that the public were becoming more aware of the unsavoury practices happening in their local churchyards. Raids had to be carried out further afield.

The populace was becoming more attuned to the level of corruption among officials, too. It was no longer possible for raids to occur on such a level, or for nearly every sexton, constable or parish watchman to be in the pay of the resurrection men. By the early 1820s, members of the Borough Gang were going their separate ways and new alliances were being made by those gang members who stayed in the profession.

The monopoly once held by the greatest bodysnatching gang in England was finally weakening and the range of opportunities available to individuals embarking on a career as a resurrectionist could not have been better.

Chapter 3

A Slick Operation
The *Modus Operandi* of the bodysnatching trade

'A singular instance of the trick played by resurrection men for the purpose of obtaining dead bodies occurred in Grub Street [London] the other day. . . the bodysnatchers set their wits on how to substitute something for a corpse and to carry off the subject before sepulture [sic].'
— *Public Ledger & Daily Advertiser,*
Wednesday, 11 February 1829.

The professional bodysnatcher had to perfect their *modus operandi* right down to the finest detail. The frequency at which anatomists required fresh cadavers, combined with the need to snatch a corpse without detection, left no margin for error. Gone were the days of leaving empty coffins strewn across the church-yard, a trail of burial clothes leading to the mouth of the grave.

With the advent of the 1816 'cutting scandal' and the inter-gang rivalry seen in the Borough Gang, smaller groups of three to four members, some including women, were emerging, as well as individual entrepreneurs. The tactics they employed in procuring cadavers demonstrated just how cunning and determined these new professionals were prepared to be.

Knowing where to dig was the first stage in efficiently procuring a dead body, although information received regarding the freshest graves was not always accurate. Peterborough bodysnatchers William Whayley and William Patrick let their nerves get the better of them the first time they ventured out on a raid in 1830. William Patrick claimed that he had resorted to the resurrecting business in order to look after his sick wife, having accepted the offer of work from a mysterious Mr Grimmer.

He said that Grimmer repeatedly called by his house offering financial help – if he would 'raise a body or two'. It did not take much for Patrick to agree; the prospect of money to a family who were 'forced to run into debt at times' was probably very welcome. Unwilling to go wandering through graveyards on his own, Patrick secured the help of his friend William Whayley, albeit after much persuasion. Their first bodysnatching attempt placed them in Peterborough burial ground at the beginning of November 1830, but after they opened the grave, it became obvious that all was not right.

'It will not do,' Patrick reportedly said, 'the man who put me into this business [Grimmer] has marked the wrong grave.' Still unnerved by their first expedition, a fortnight later the pair attempted to steal a cadaver from Yaxley churchyard, nearly five miles south of Peterborough. With the promise of half a sovereign if the snatching came off, the two carefully made their way to the marked grave. The two men were by no means professionals. After digging down to the coffin – and having to hide in the grave whilst the watch fired randomly across the churchyard – Patrick was unable to break the lid sufficiently to extract the corpse. 'You try to pull the corpse out whilst I lift the lid up,' Patrick suggested to Whayley. 'I cannot,' said Whayley 'You come here then and take my place and I'll take yours,' and so it happened that Patrick pulled the corpse out of the grave with his bare hands and stuffed it into a sack, which was thrown onto Whayley's back.

The body of Jane Mason was then concealed in a hut belonging to the local surgeon, Mr Johnson, to be collected at a later hour. But Jane was found tied up in the sack, and mistakenly identified as 23-year-old Elizabeth Billings. During discussions with witnesses and the relatives of the deceased in order to confirm the identity of the corpse, a letter arrived addressed to the local surgeon stating that the body could not possibly be that of Elizabeth Billings, for she had already been dissected and that the body lying in front of them was from Yaxley churchyard. The letter had been sent by none other than Mr Grimmer, who had fled Peterborough when Jane's corpse had been discovered.

Although both Patrick and Whayley were indicted for 'violating the sanctity of the grave', Whayley turned King's evidence. Patrick pleaded guilty to the indictment and received twelve months' imprisonment.

Casually sauntering around a village, taking in the perimeter of the churchyard and keeping a look out for freshly dug graves was one of the easiest ways of finding out whether a churchyard might be worth visiting later that night. Many later apprehended bodysnatchers, were reportedly seen leaning against the churchyard wall, observing the sexton at his work prior to their crime.

Details such as nature of death were also important, if the deceased had been mangled in an accident then the body would be worthless to the anatomists. The main problem with scouting out potential graves in the provinces was that in such tight-knit communities the presence of a stranger was almost certain to be noticed and widely remarked upon.

When the grave of Catherine Mack was being dug in the parish church of Prestonkirk, East Lothian in January 1819, Jane Frizzel, the wife of the local gravedigger, noted 'two strange men in the churchyard right above the grave'. John Kerr, George McLaren and George Campbell were subsequently convicted of attempting to 'violate the sepulchre'. Three bodysnatchers, two men and one woman, also caught the attention of the locals in Crail, Fife, shortly before New Year's Eve 1823, after they were seen loitering around the churchyard. Suspecting that their cover had been blown, the three perpetrators left the area rather more rapidly than they had intended.

Unknown women would perhaps cause less suspicion in the parish, for their presence could be more easily explained away, perhaps with the claim of being a long-lost relative of the deceased. A favourite story was that the young lady, having just heard of the demise of her 'once very dear uncle' had come as quickly as she could to attend his funeral. In reality, the young lady was scouring the churchyard for potential graves to target.

A scout might note any anti-bodysnatching devices used, such as cemetery guns or make a mental note of any personal tokens placed on top of the grave. These were often used by the poorer members of the parish as a way of indicating that a grave had been tampered with. Reports would then be sent back to the bodysnatchers, so that any prevention methods could be dealt with and a plan hatched.

In 1827, an article in the *Hampshire Chronicle* noted a new method employed by the bodysnatchers:

'when an individual dies suddenly, whose name is unknown to the parish authorities, the deceased is of course advertised, to discover his friends. A well-dressed female is soon employed by the resurrection men to claim him as a relative; who, on being indulged with a sight of the corpse, exhibits a paroxysm of grief, attend every symptom of the most tender affection and regret.'

A gang of resurrectionists working in Devonport, Manchester during 1830 included three men and two women. A house behind the local churchyard was hired on a yearly basis. It was furnished handsomely and became the base for the whole party. The women played their role perfectly, making 'discreet' enquiries as to the ages of the recently deceased and to the causes of death. Unfortunately, their enquiries happened to be made the day after neighbours had alerted the parish constable to the suspicious activities going on at the house, and the large number of packages being carried away from the property.

By attending the same funeral as the two women, the constable hoped to gather evidence against the gang and he was not disappointed. He watched the women return to the house and came back later that evening, positioning several parties in different parts of the churchyard, successfully arresting the whole gang whilst they were engaged in bodysnatching. When the house was searched two sacks were discovered, one containing the body of an 18-year-old female, the other an 54-year-old male.

How did a bodysnatcher go about removing a cadaver from a coffin buried six feet below ground? In order to carry out the operation quickly and effectively, special techniques needed to be developed. To extract a corpse, there was no need for anyone to stand in the grave, throwing soil over their shoulders, hoping that it would not be too long before they heard the thud of their spade hitting the coffin lid. As a general rule, bodysnatchers did not remove much soil when exhuming a body, yet there were many assumptions as to how they worked. Some believed that the bodysnatcher would dig the entire coffin out of the grave and replace it once the body had been removed.

Others, like Thomas Wakley, the founder of the medical journal *The Lancet*, envisaged a more skilled operation:

'Several feet – fifteen or twenty – away from the head or foot of the grave, he would remove a square of turf, about eighteen or twenty inches in diameter. This he would carefully put by, and then commence to mine. . . Taking a five foot grave, the coffin lid would be about four feet from the surface. A rough slanting tunnel, some five yards long, would therefore have to be constructed, so as to impinge exactly on the coffin head. This being at last struck . . . the coffin was lugged by hooks to the surface, or preferably, the end of the coffin was wretched with hooks while still in the shelter of the tunnel, and the scalp or feet of the corpse secured through the open end, and the body pulled out, leaving the coffin almost intact and unmoved. The body once obtained, the narrow shaft easily filled up and the sod of turf accurately replaced.'

Wakley's account, written in 1823, would not have been practical. Digging a tunnel in soil that had not already been disturbed would have been too time-consuming and arduous. If this was the method used, how could upwards of five or six bodies be snatched in one evening? The real method of exhumation was much swifter and, if everything worked in the resurrectionists' favour, a body could be extracted from a coffin in about an hour.

However, an evening's bodysnatching would often commence after the group had consumed a number of alcoholic beverages. Not only was a strong stomach needed for the job in hand, but most bodysnatchers welcomed the blurring of their senses once the coffin lid was removed.

Thomas Wilkinson Wallis, a one-time patient at Hull Medical School, recalled in his autobiography that, whilst recovering from surgery, he accidentally became party to conversations in adjoining rooms regaling the tales of the bodysnatchers. He recalled 'a tall, gaunt man frequently [coming] to the surgery for glasses of strong spirits of wine, the gin retailed at the inns not [being] strong enough for him.' Escaping corpse gases it seemed could knock even the most hardened of bodysnatcher for six.

Having reached the grave, either by climbing over the churchyard wall or having paid the sexton to leave the churchyard gate open, the resurrectionist's first task was to identify the 'head end' of the coffin. Once this had been done, the digging could commence. Laying a sack alongside the grave to catch any excess soil and to prevent it from marking the grass, the team could set about moving the soil from the top end of the grave to the foot – this was advantageous once they got down to breaking the coffin lid.

Wooden spades were used, as iron ones made too much noise when they struck any stones. Using a couple of iron hooks or a crowbar, the bodysnatchers would then tug at the coffin lid. The lid would naturally snap at the corpse's shoulders, because of the weight of the soil handily placed further down the coffin. Sacking would also be placed on top of the coffin to deaden the sound of the splitting wood. Standing aside to let the corpse gasses escape, they could then begin to place ropes either around the corpse's head or under its armpits. On the count of three, the cadaver could be pulled free of the coffin – 'a jerking movement is said to have been more effective than violent dragging' – stripped of its grave clothes and squashed into a sack.

Targeting a pauper's grave involved a slightly different approach. Typically, pauper graves contained more than one burial – and in the eyes of the bodysnatcher, this could equate to quite a reasonable haul. As all the coffins would be buried to the same depth, all that was required was to remove the loose soil and concentrate on opening each coffin individually.

Three bodysnatchers, Thomas Shearing, William Thames and Thomas Kelly, were brought before Spitalfields watch-house in October 1823 and charged with trying to steal two dead bodies from the paupers' burial ground in St James, Clerkenwell. The attempt was doomed from the outset. Concerned neighbours had noticed that the casement of a window, which happened to overlook the burial ground, had been removed and a curtain put up in its place. This naturally attracted some attention, causing people to wonder whether an attempt to steal away dead bodies might be made following a burial the previous day.

With a watch in place, the bodysnatchers were allowed to proceed with part of their plan, in the hope that they would then be caught red-handed. After tying one body up in a sack, the gang caught wind that they were being watched and attempted to escape. Their only escape route however, was to scale a 30ft high wall surrounding the burial ground which, on the side the gang chose, fell away to the Fleet Ditch. Having successfully reached the top of the wall, there was nowhere left to turn and the men plunged 'up to their necks in the mud and filth of the river'.

That same year, four 'body-stealers' were apprehended in the early hours of Sunday, 13 April, having targeted the pauper burial ground at the back of the workhouse in Shoe Lane, London. The burial ground had 'only one depository' – a large hole capable of holding over one hundred coffins. As a way of deterring the bodysnatchers, a large piece of iron, weighing nearly 800lbs and requiring a pulley to lift it up and down, had been placed over the hole.

This proved no obstacle for the bodysnatchers, for not only did they manage to remove the piece of iron and carry out a raid on the churchyard, they also broke a secure padlock from an iron bar used to hold down wooden flaps along-side the paupers' grave and replace it with one of their own for easier and regular access.

Yet, the watch was aware of their activities and the watchmen waited for the bodysnatchers to make their way over the graveyard wall with their tools, remove the iron bar from across the grave and then split into two groups. Two of the resurrection men made for the wall to keep watch, whilst the others leapt into the hole. Immediately the watchmen sprang into action, the wooden flaps on the paupers' grave were closed and the iron bar replaced, trapping two of the bodysnatchers in the grave. The other two made their escape over the wall and were apprehended in a house alongside the burial ground. The cries of the bodysnatchers trapped in the grave were eventually answered after half-an-hour, when all four men were apprehended in the watch-house for questioning.

What would happen supposing a group of bodysnatchers had found a suitable grave to target later, but noticed that the grave was rigged? Trip wires might lead to a cemetery gun or the watch could be in position nearby, waiting for bodysnatchers to climb over the wall. All was not lost, however, traps just added a little more danger to the operation. Tokens placed on top of the grave by those who couldn't afford mortsafes or iron coffins, would be noted by bodysnatchers' scouts and it was a simple matter of replacing them in the exact same location once the grave had been refilled.

The watch and/or sextons could in many cases be paid off in advance or their attention might be diverted in some way. Corruption came in many different forms and examples of officials in the pay of bodysnatchers can be found across the country. Bribing sextons to make the cadaver more accessible prior to burial was a common method used by the bodysnatchers.

The *Derby Mercury* printed a short report as late as 1859, detailing a bribe that a bodysnatcher, thought to have been from Sheffield, had apparently offered the former sexton of Brampton Church, Derbyshire. However, the promise of a sovereign failed to tempt him and soon word got round the parish that an attempt was to be made on the recently interred bodies of two females. After putting a watch on the churchyard and vicinity for a number of days, the body-snatcher failed to make an appearance.

The sexton of the burial ground attached to The Royal Hospital in Haslar, Hampshire was certainly more susceptible to making money by collaborating with bodysnatchers. William Seymour lived in a house close to the burial ground and was employed as the sexton at the hospital. On 26 December 1824, Seymour offered the body of a mariner Thomas Brookland, who had died from hepatitis to bodysnatchers John Johnson and Henry Andrews, who were reportedly in the habit of travelling from London to Portsmouth, in order to ship bodies back to the capital. Johnson and Andrews were caught at the Star Inn, Portsea, after a trunk they were waiting for was discovered to contain Thomas Brookland's body. Wishing to confirm his suspicions, the constable at the scene requested that the trunk be opened in the tap room of the inn. 'For God's sake man,' Johnson reportedly said. 'Don't open it, there's a dead body, and I shall be torn to pieces by the people.'

During the trial, it transpired that Seymour had been involved in the exhumation of four bodies from the Haslar burial ground, all of which had been for Johnson and Andrews. Seymour had received thirty shillings and 'plenty of gin and beer' for his helpful role in the operation.

The judge, Mr Justice Borough was so appalled by the crime that he declared he would do his best to put a stop to this 'crime of the foulest character'. Because of the lack of evidence proving Henry Andrews' involvement in the snatchings, he was acquitted, but the fate of Johnson and Seymour was not to be as favourable. Johnson was sentenced to six months' imprisonment and fined fifty pounds. As for William Seymour, he was too poor to pay a fine and so he was sentenced to twelve months' imprisonment instead.

An Exeter surgeon William Cooke received a much higher fine of £100 for employing sexton Giles Yard to obtain a body for him to dissect. Yard was charged along with Cooke for having stolen the body of Elizabeth Taylor from the churchyard of St David's, Exeter. The day after Elizabeth's funeral, her son Thomas Jerrard, examined his mother's grave, having heard rumours about a possible snatching. To his horror he found both the grave and coffin open and the body missing. There had been a frost that evening and Jerrard noticed footprints leading from the coffin to Yard's house in St Mary Arches Lane.

After entering the premises with constables, Jerrard found the body of his mother laid out on a table covered with a white cloth. Yard was arrested after his shoe was found to match one of the sets of prints at the graveside. Other accounts state that it was Yard himself who raised the alarm, perhaps to remove suspicion from himself. Either way, the evidence was stacking up against the pair, for not only did Yard's footprints match those discovered at the scene, but a spade was also located in his house covered in clay similar to that found in Elizabeth's grave.

After deliberating for over three hours the jury found both Cooke and Yard guilty. While Cooke received a fine, Giles Yard was unable to pay his bail and so was committed to Exeter Gaol for a term of nine months, until he was discharged by order of the King's Bench. Cooke and Yard were also charged with stealing the clothes of the deceased, which was classed as a felony. Stealing a cadaver did not carry the same weight as stealing grave clothes. In the eyes of the law a cadaver was not considered to be real property, yet grave clothes were, hence the theft of such items carried a higher penalty. In the case of Cooke and Yard, however, there was not sufficient evidence to prove that they had actually stolen any grave clothes and this side of their case was dropped.

As professional bodysnatching intensified, some snatchers became bolder in their attempts to secure cadavers and cases were reported in which bodies had been stolen from private houses whilst the deceased was waiting to be buried. Hoxton, London was the target of such a daring attempt in 1828, according to a report in the *Morning Post*.

Two resurrection men, Phillips and Longman, were charged with breaking into 2 Queen's Head Walk, the home of the recently widowed Mrs Parrot. During the night in question, Mrs Parrot and her daughter awoke to a strange noise in the parlour and upon investigating, Mrs Parrot noticed that the parlour window had been smashed and that her husband's body had been partially stripped of his grave clothes. Despite being 'screwed down in his coffin' and in the secure environment of his home, Mr Parrot was still a target for the opportunist bodysnatchers.

'Dead body stealer' William Jones was also caught trying to remove the corpse of a 14-year-old girl from a house in Shoreditch in 1831. Jones was caught due to the fact that he had been seen coming out of the house with a basket, which 'contained something that smelt very offensive'.

In response to the increasingly bold bodysnatchers, the watch devised more deadly deterrents, such as the cemetery gun. This was a gun rigged with trip wires and positioned over the grave, so that it would go off if the grave was tampered with. In 1823, bodysnatchers targeted the burial ground in Camden Town and were caught on Holborn Hill, transporting four bodies in the back of a cart. The bodies were identified as four paupers who had recently passed away in the St Martin in the Fields Workhouse.

Interestingly, when the Camden gravedigger gave his statement in court he stated that although he had known 'the bodies had been stolen, he had kept the secret to himself'. Rather than alerting the officials, instead he refilled the graves so that they appeared undisturbed. The bodysnatchers had dismantled the wires on the cemetery guns and simply thrown them back into the grave when refilling it. The gravedigger knowing this, unearthed the guns, reset them and 'made the grave complete again,' in the hope that 'the matter might not be talked about'. Was this another gravedigger in the pay of the bodysnatcher or was he merely eager to avoid scandal?

A slightly more extreme example of a grave being protected by a cemetery gun was reported in *The Times* in 1817. The highly-sought-after corpse of a 7ft tall grenadier had been buried in the churchyard of St Martin in the Fields. Knowing that an attempt to purloin his unusual corpse would soon be made by the bodysnatchers, the sexton 'put together a number of gun barrels, so as to form a magazine, that they might all be discharged together.'

The apparatus was rigged so that the muzzle was directed straight at the grave, and a string was fixed to the trigger with the other end attached to a piece of wood. The wood was then buried in the grave about a foot below the surface. As soon as digging commenced, whoever was holding the spade would come across the piece of wood and have to move it. When the wood was touched, the trigger would be pulled and 'a volley of bullets would immediately sweep that quarter of the burying ground'.

At about 4.30am on 30 December, the sexton heard 'a tremendous report' and quickly made his way in to the churchyard, where he found 'spades, shovels, picks and other resurrection paraphernalia'. He also found a man's hat with a bullet hole in one side of it. As there was no exit hole, the sexton concluded that it must have lodged in the head of one of the bodysnatchers, killing him instantly, with his friends taking his lifeless body away with them. No record has been found of what happened to the body of the unfortunate resurrectionist, but one can perhaps surmise that his colleagues received a good price for him.

Aside from the risks involved in stealing a corpse, there was also the possibility that it might not be quite as fresh as anticipated. In such cases the snatch could still be salvaged, for body parts were just as profitable as a whole cadaver. If a body was too putrid, then a less decomposed part could be cut off and the extremities, such as the arms and legs, might still be used in demonstrations.

Originally a gravedigger at St James's Church, Clerkenwell, Joseph Naples was known for cutting off extremities, removing them from partially decomposed bodies so that they could be sold separately. An entry in Naples's diary dated 27 February 1812, shows that such body parts were sold to St Thomas' Hospital. Another entry from 12 August 1812 reveals that the gang 'cut off the extremitys [sic] took to Bartholm[ews] [Hospital]', receiving one pound for them. In August 1812, the gang dug up a corpse that was too 'decomposed to bring away', but it wasn't a completely wasted effort, for 'they drew the canine teeth and sold them'. A month later they were not quite so lucky when they failed to sell a cadaver to St Thomas' Hospital because it was deemed too putrid.

The desire to have specific body parts, either for anatomical collections or to investigate the veins and muscles beneath, was not confined to the surgeons of London, as one story recounted in *A History of Bristol Infirmary* shows. It reveals that the severed head of a recently deceased patient of Bristol Infirmary was lost one evening. As medical students John Danvers and Richard Smith made their way back from the dead house, the head was carefully wrapped and concealed under Danvers's coat. The pair had removed it from the body in preparation for a lecture on the brain. When Danvers accidentally knocked his elbow on a wall, he lost his grip on the severed head, which fell with a thud on to the ground and rolled away in the direction of a nearby bush.

Unable to find the head and fearing that their crime might soon be detected, the pair made their way back to their rooms empty-handed. After fortifying themselves with brandy, they devised a plan to retrieve their 'goods'. The two gentlemen decided they would simply link arms and walk 'backwards and forwards until [they] have [covered] the whole space thereabout, pretending that [they] were merely walking and conversing for amusement'. The plan worked and after about an hour Danvers's foot struck something round and hard. On this occasion the anatomists escaped the authorities but it is unclear if they learnt anything from their close shave.

For those in the know, teeth could turn a very handsome profit indeed and would always be taken out of the corpse and sold separately before the body was handed over to the anatomists. A gang of resurrectionists consisting of three men and two women, operating in Plymouth and Devonport, were found in possession of teeth which 'must have belonged to fifteen or sixteen human bodies.' This would have made them a very handsome profit on top of the money they made from the cadavers.

During the early nineteenth century, teeth were removed on the battlefields of the Peninsular War by 'wrenching and twisting with pincers in hand' and made into dentures. Tom Butler, a member of the Crouch Gang, is said to have made £300 on just one trip to the battlefields, during which he collected teeth from the dead and dying. When demand for cadavers was low during the summer months, Joseph Naples also dealt in teeth and could earn a guinea for a full set.

A gravedigger by the name of James Foxley was tried at Warwickshire Quarter Sessions in July 1826 for 'violating and disturb[ing] the remains of nineteen year old Jonathan Bedford in a Birmingham churchyard.' A little girl had seen Foxley at Bedford's graveside the morning after his funeral and had told the chapel wardens that she thought the grave looked as though it was open. When

Bedford's grave was re-opened, the coffin had indeed been broken, but to everyone's surprise the body was still there.

However, it was not the flesh that Foxley had been after, for dissection lectures had finished for the season by then. It was Bedford's teeth that had taken his fancy and Bedford's head had been 'shockingly cut and mangled' in order to remove the teeth from his jaws. When questioned as to why he'd been digging in Bedford's grave, Foxley replied that he had lost his rope and that had been looking for it. This improbable story did not wash and Foxley was found guilty, sentenced to three months' imprisonment.

Once a resurrectionist had a cadaver in their procession, what would they do with it? There were two primary destinations for the corpse: the local anatomist's slab or to be trussed up like a chicken and stuffed into a heavily disguised receptacle, ready for shipment elsewhere. If the delivery was local, there were a number of different transportation options available, some more discreet than others. Perhaps bodysnatcher Alexander Lyons was not aware of this when he brazenly walked up the back steps of Sheffield Music Hall in 1831, en-route to the lecture rooms of the Medical Hall with the corpse of 33-year-old William Hopkinson slung over his shoulder. Discretion and concealment played a key part in the whole operation.

Bodies were transported in sacks, barrows and even passed off as drunken friends, all in the name of science. Tales of bodysnatchers transporting bodies across the country conjure up images of a criminal underworld in which a fight or flight attitude was required. Transporting a body through the back streets of Hull in 1832 drew attention to two bodysnatchers when a corpse was found tied up in a sack in the back of a gig in Charles Street. Nineteen-old Michael Wallis and 37-year old William Jones were both apprehended at the scene, Wallis after being seen unlocking the door of the dissecting room.

The dead man was found in the back of their cart, tied up in a sack with his head poking out of the top. He was later identified as William Butler, recently interred at Myton burial ground in Kingston upon Hull. Despite walking alongside the cart whilst it travelled along Charles Street, Wallis was adamant that he did not know Jones. He claimed that the reason that he held a key to the dissecting rooms was because he did 'little jobs' for the medical men – he was in fact employed as a cleaner at the school. Both men were tried at the January 1833 sessions and sentenced to two months' imprisonment.

1833 was a busy year for bodysnatchers in Hull, for two further resurrection men were tried at the same sessions as Wallis and Jones. William Ware, a notorious bodysnatcher, who also answered to the alias 'Edinburgh Bill', was brought to trial together with George Newton for stealing the body of 37-year-old Sarah Harper from her grave in Cottingham churchyard.

Witness Joseph Noblett had double-crossed the two bodysnatchers, for Ware, having invited Noblett to stay at his house, had persuaded him to join them in a number of bodysnatching forays. Agreeing to be on board, but having previously alerted the Hull constables, Noblett made his way to Cottingham churchyard, along with Ware.

Having watched Ware uncover Sarah's coffin and break open the lid, he was surprised to hear that Ware had 'only intended to take the head and a leg, but as the body was in good order, he would take it altogether and if not sold at Beverley, would send it to Edinburgh'. Ware exclaimed that if he had a mind to, he could get a guinea for the teeth too, but for some reason he chose not to remove them straight away. He did however cut off Sarah's hair which he boasted he could sell for a shilling in Hull. Some of Sarah's hair would be produced later as part of the evidence against Ware.

The box that Sarah was squashed into measured 25in by 16in and was 16in deep. From the label stuck to the side of the box, it was to be directed to 'Mr Lizar, by Carlisle, Edinbro' (glass)'. Indeed, when Ware and Newton were arrested, Ware was carrying a letter from an Edinburgh surgeon which read:

'*Edinburgh, Brown Square 14 Sept 1832*- I received your last letter, and I shall be very happy to receive some from you. If you can pack them well, and send via Carlisle, they will come safe. If you send them by Newcastle they will be stopped – Write me before you send them when I may expect them, and I will return you the money the moment I receive them. They must be sent by coach. Hope to hear from you . . . Signed Liz.'

A Dr John Lizars did practice in Edinburgh at this time and, interestingly, had once also employed Daniel Butler, a former superintendent of the dissecting room at St Thomas' Hospital, London, and also a one-time member of the Crouch gang. Ware and Newton were both found guilty and each received twelve months' imprisonment.

It is rare to get a glimpse into the personal life of a bodysnatcher, but when *The Hull Packet and Humber Mercury* ran the story of the trial, they embellished it with a little more detail than usual. It was noted that Ware 'has lately been living with the notorious 'Mrs Sutton', who had been committed 'for a felony, on Saturday week'. Ann Sutton's case is recorded in the criminal registers for the County of York, where she was convicted of felony at the same quarter sessions as Ware and Newton.

Ann Sutton (alias Sparrow, alias Johnson, alias Ware) was indicted for stealing surgical instruments, including a silver probe and a pair of steel forceps, all of which belonged to Henry Snowden, an apprentice in Sculcoates. Unfortunately for Ware, Ann would not be around when he was released from gaol, for she was transported for seven years, declaring to the judge that she was 'much obliged' when she heard of her sentence.

One story, which has no doubt been exaggerated over the years, concerns two Glasgow medical students who targeted the churchyard at Mearns, south of Glasgow in the first few years of 1800. Their ingenious idea was to disguise the corpse as a friend. The 'friend' had unfortunately become sick during their journey and the students were naturally keen to get him back to their lodgings as quickly as possible.

With the corpse propped up between the two healthy students on the seat at the front of a gig, the journey home took them through the Gorbals tollbar where they were expected to stop and pay the required fee. Fearing that they were about to be sprung, the two students pulled off quite a remarkable ruse, for as one student counted out the toll money, the other put his arm around his 'friend', highlighting the fact that he was unwell and proceeded to mop his brow! The keeper of the tollbar was sympathetic and, after passing a few kind words to the 'trio', advised them to 'drive cannily hame, lads, drive cannily'. The students had just successfully passed off a corpse as a living human being.

* * *

As cadavers were shipped to the teaching hospitals and private anatomy schools across England and Scotland, bodysnatchers therefore required the assistance of a coach or smack, a traditional fishing boat, in order to supply a large number of major towns and cities.

A major hazard during transportation was the tell-tale odour of the corpse revealing what was being transported. The smell emitted from one of the boxes that arrived at the Talbot Coach Office in Manchester one November day in 1831, ensured that it was removed from the coach and examined. Sure enough it contained a body, this time of an elderly man, ready to be sent to a fictitious recipient, 'Major Wood, Carlisle'.

Cases of bodies being discovered in transit due to their offensive smell appeared quite often in the newspapers. The trussed-up body of Mary Ann Roberts, about to be transported on the London bound Union Coach in 1831, was discovered at The Red Lion Inn, Banbury because passengers waiting to board noticed the 'offensive smell' from the box. With 'their nasal organs assailed by a most disagreeable stench', the luggage was examined to try to find the cause of the odour. Mary Ann had already travelled over two and a half miles from Broughton, Oxfordshire before she was discovered.

Banbury Gaol records show that a Joseph Terrill (Tyrell) was charged on 20 October with stealing the body of Mary Ann Roberts the previous day. Failing to find sureties, Terrill was removed to Oxford Gaol at 4am five days later, where he served a twelve-month sentence.

The smell emanating from a trunk deposited at the Telegraph coach offices at The Rampant Horse Inn, Norwich, in the summer of 1823 was enough for suspicions to be aroused and countryman Ephraim Ulph apprehended after he tried to deliver the trunk.

Further investigations led to two London bodysnatchers, Thomas Crowe and Joseph Nichols Collins, who had paid Ulph sixpence for taking the trunk to the coach office. When the box, measuring 28in by 13in and 12in deep and wrapped in paper, was opened to determine its contents, the naked body of James Brundall, recently interred in Lackenham Churchyard was discovered, his head lodged between his feet so that he could fit snugly inside the trunk.

A search was made of Crowe's lodgings and a number of other incriminating discoveries were made. Two teeth were discovered which, in surgeon Mr Robinson's expert opinion, fitted exactly into 'apertures in the gums of the corpse'. A set of thirteen skeleton keys were also found, with an additional two keys discovered at Collins's abode. A shovel, sack and 'old dirty wearing apparel, stiff with mold' a length of rope and some screwdrivers had been found in a nearby stable rented by Crowe.

The keys were perhaps the main piece of evidence against the pair. When the keys were tried in church doors within the neighbourhood, five churches out of seven were easily entered. The bodysnatchers had also known of Brundall's burial, as they had been spotted standing in different parts of the churchyard during the funeral. There was no denying that Crowe and Collins were the culprits and they were both found guilty following their trial. The sentence for both men was the same: a fifty-pound fine and three months in Norwich Gaol.

Having stolen a cadaver, bodysnatchers were not always in a position to deliver it immediately to its final destination. When men employed to gather hay in the Hampstead Road area of London stuck their pitchfork into some hay lying under a rick one November morning in 1818, they were surprised to hit a hard object. Gingerly reaching into the hay, one of the men discovered a dead body and, after reaching in for a second time, another body was found.

A year later, the bodies of two children were recovered from a dung heap in Sutton, near Reigate and taken to the Red Lion Public House for examination. Upon investigation, it was discovered that notorious bodysnatchers Joseph Naples and George Marden had been spotted near the churchyard with a horse and cart. (It is possible that George Marden was the bodysnatcher George Martin, another member of the Borough Gang.)

Their crime having gone undetected, the pair had made their way peacefully to the Red Lion for a drink. The landlord of the pub checked the back of their cart, only to find 'implements as are used by resurrection men'. Unfortunately for Naples and Marden, they were also later seen near the dung heap and, fearing they had been detected, the pair fled, leaving their horse and cart behind.

One of the most alarming stories relating to bodysnatchers stashing corpses until they could be safely whisked away occurred in Islington in 1821. After a number of human limbs were found floating in the Regents Canal, two surgeons appeared on the scene and brazenly proceeded to try to cut off a leg whilst constables were still gathering the naked cadavers from the water. When set upon by the gathering crowd, the two men stated that they were in fact surgeons and that 'the bodies had been there deposited by the resurrection men.'

To get an adult body to fit into a box or hamper was no mean feat. Tucking the feet behind the head and tying securely in place may have worked on occasion, but human bodies come in a variety of shapes and sizes and naturally required different vessels. Discoveries of bodies concealed in varied types of containers were often reported, some accounts being embellished with rather specific details.

When a hamper was delayed at Downe's Wharf, London in 1815 during its transfer to Edinburgh, workers noticed a 'bad smell' emanating from it whilst it was being moved aboard the *Leith* smack. Turning the hamper round a number of times to try to find the cause of the stench, the bottom gave way and a hand fell out on to the deck. Perhaps the men on board began to wish they hadn't been so inquisitive, but they decided to open the hamper fully in order to take a closer look.

With the lid off there was no denying what lay before them:

> 'A naked body of a man was found, with his head bent back behind his shoulders, his tongue cut out, and his belly sewed up; both the feet cut a little above the ancles [sic] and the other parts of the legs and thighs were bent up to the belly, to put the whole of the body in a small compass. The tongue and feet were not found and the body altogether was in a putrid state.'

There were no signs on the body of it having been buried and, although consideration was given to this being the work of the resurrection men, the coroner returned a verdict of wilful murder by person or persons unknown. The question is, however, why had the body been packed into a hamper and labelled for removal to Edinburgh and why, if a murder victim, was the corpse in such a decomposed state?

In a similar case in 1826, workers at George's Dock, Liverpool also became suspicious when loading barrels labelled 'Bitter Salts' onto the smack *Latona*. In all, eleven bodies would be found after the master of the vessel, Mr Walker, removed a small bundle of straw in the side of one of the barrels and thrust his hand into the hole. The barrels contained the cadavers of men and women, pickled and packed in a variety of arrangements. The first barrel contained one male and two female corpses, the second two males and one female and the last three males and one female. The bodies were heading to Leith to supply Edinburgh medical students with subjects to dissect.

The discovery at George's Dock exposed one of the largest organisations of 'wholesale resurrectionists' ever found. Their base at Hope Street, Liverpool unearthed a further twenty-two bodies all in various stages of packing. Men, women and children of all ages were discovered in sacks and casks, some of which were also filled with salt to aid preservation.

On examining three casks and three sacks found in the house, local surgeon Thomas William Davies noted:

'Nine men, five women, five boys and three girls. Total number of bodies thirty three. The bodies were whole and in a perfect state. Those in the casks appeared to have been dead six or seven days; those in the sacks might have been dead two or three days. The whole of the bodies were entirely naked; there was not the least mark of any external violence on them; nor was there any reason to suppose that the persons had not died a natural death . . . the remains of a thread on the toes of one of the young women (which practice is used, in some families, to keep the feet of the deceased together) [suggests] that the bodies had been disinterred.'

Three men were found to be involved in the Hope Street affair, although only two were arrested. At the next Liverpool Quarter Sessions James Donaldson and John Henderson were charged with 'disinterring a number of dead bodies', which was categorised as a misdemeanour. The charge against the third body-snatcher William Gillespie, a blacksmith by trade, was ignored. Twenty-five-year-old James Donaldson was fined fifty pounds and sentenced to twelve months' imprisonment in Kirkdale Gaol. The ringleader, John Henderson recorded as a cooper from Greenock, Scotland, disappeared before the trial and was never caught.

As in the Hope Street case, cadavers would be squashed and packed into barrels and labelled as 'Pickled Herrings', 'Bitter Salts' or 'Crystal' and labelled with a false name and address, or even with instructions to 'hold until called for.'

Newspaper reports of these grisly discoveries were usually very detailed and gave sufficient information for the reader to conjure up an image of the horror involved in their mind's eye. In 1798 the body of a 'fine limbed young lady' was found in a box, when William Gray was stopped in Snow Fields, London. In order to fit her body into the box, Gray had 'tied [her] neck and hams together'. Another female corpse was found in 1815, 'doubled up, like a fish in a basket', in the back of London hackney coach No. 569.

Bodies would be packed in sawdust to prevent movement and to absorb any liquids that might seep from the corpse. Careful packing did not help the body of a 19-year-old woman go undetected at the Turf Hotel, Newcastle in 1825, for 'a most nauseous smell was felt from a liquid oozing therefrom'.

One Sunday evening in 1830, a man's hand was found protruding from the stream in Long Benton, Newcastle. The hand was attached to the corpse of Martin Hall who had been stuffed into a sack about two days previously and put into the water ready for collection later. Hall's ears and nostrils had carefully been stuffed with tow (flax/hemp fibres).

Operating from the immediate neighbourhood lessened the chance of a body-snatcher being caught on the open road in possession of a naked corpse. In 1818, a 'stranger' rented a house in Fox Court, Ray Street, backing on to the St James's burial ground in Clerkenwell. Neighbours kept careful watch on the stranger, noting that he was generally away from home late at night, when a series of strange noises would be heard from inside the house.

Their suspicions were confirmed when a little girl, who had been playing next door, peered through a hole in the wall and saw the body of a naked man stretched out upon the floor. Although only one corpse was found to be in the house after it was searched, it was alongside 'all the necessary implements' used for body-snatching, such as a sack, cords and spades. Six coffins in the nearby graveyard were found to be empty and the involvement of the gravedigger, who was seen levelling soil on top of the graves at an early hour, did not go unnoticed.

Five years later, another stranger also rented a house in Fox's Court on Ray Street, the window of which still looked over the burial ground. The body-snatcher, John Lawrence – described by the *Morning Chronicle* as 'one of the most notorious resurrection men known' – had rented the property for five shillings per week giving the alias John Gore. When apprehended he reportedly had 'very dirty [knees] from fresh soil, as if he had been kneeling on the ground'. The body of a man, believed to have died ten days prior in the workhouse, was also found tied in a sack within the house, all ready for the anatomist's table.

The same names repeatedly crop up in bodysnatching cases. A John Lawrence was sentenced to twelve months' imprisonment at the Somerset Lent assizes in 1830 for stealing dead bodies. Lawrence was apprehended with Joseph Madden, an 'old offender', after being found with three bodies in their possession (one female and two male) all of which had been stuffed into a cask of oil.

Joseph Madden had previously been apprehended with another known bodysnatcher, William Clarke (alias Taylor), in 1826. The assize report in the *Salisbury and Winchester Journal*, dated 10 April, stated that Clarke 'had been tried twenty eight times for this offense [sic] before', and had 'been accustomed to the resurrection business since he was six years of age'. He received a sentence of twelve months' imprisonment, along with a one hundred pound fine, for stealing dead bodies from Walcot Churchyard, Bath.

In order to gain better access to the churchyard, Clarke had rented a house in which the back windows overlooked the churchyard. No mention of Joseph Madden on this occasion appears in the press, but a petition relating to Clarke's imprisonment in 1826 requesting grounds for clemency survives in The National Archives. The petition is signed by seventeen members of the London College of Surgeons and one sentence in particular shows just how inadequate the legal supply of cadavers had become:

> 'the practice of dissecting is issentially [sic] necessary to the study and practice of medicine and surgery and that as no legal mode exists of procuring bodies for that purpose your petitioner has been guilty of a crime against the law but has at his own peril assisted in the useful object of a profession, whose occupation is the preservation of life, and the elevation of human misery'

With the increase in the demand for cadavers, the once secret raids in city churchyards were beginning to be noticed. The public were becoming more vigilant as to the events occurring on their own doorstep and in order to ensure there was a continual supply of cadavers for the anatomists, bodysnatchers ended up travelling further afield, visiting parishes that once considered themselves immune.

Bodysnatching was no longer confined to the inner cities. Although the majority of subjects may have ended up on the dissecting tables of London, Edinburgh and Glasgow, the practice had spread throughout England and Scotland.

The penalties received by the bodysnatchers who were apprehended did little to deter even the most nervous of resurrection men. Surgeons would step in and pay any fines administered by the court or provide for the bodysnatchers' families whilst they were in prison.

As a result of the mounting number of cases and grim newspaper coverage, the populace was becoming increasingly more concerned for the safety of departed loved ones. The violating of sepulchres had gone on long enough and they were determined to see that the practice of bodysnatching was eradicated – at least from their own small corner of the kingdom.

Rich and poor alike had a common cause in attempting to protect their dead from the clutches of the bodysnatchers by whatever means possible.

Chapter 4

Preventative Measures
The art of keeping your loved ones safe

'A great ferment has been caused in Manchester during the last week, by the detection of two Resurrection Men, and finding in their possession, no less than six human bodies, recently disinterred.'
– *Liverpool Mercury*, Friday, 27 February 1824.

Churches used many methods to deter bodysnatchers. A number of churchyards across England and Scotland went through dramatic alterations when a rumour of bodysnatching was on the lips of parishioners.

Preventative measures to combat bodysnatching were introduced mainly during the first half of nineteenth century, but prior to this city and county churchyards were often noisome, overcrowded places. Ballast Hills Burial Ground in Newcastle was the recipient of many cadavers later found stuffed into boxes which were intercepted at the Turf Hotel. In addition to the 600–800 parishioners it dealt with annually, the numerous additional bodies of the 'unknown dead' worsened the conditions within the already congested burial ground.

It was widely known that 'the portions of ground so appropriated have been literally crowded with the dead,' reported the *Newcastle Courant* in 1829, when Rev. R Pengilly was speaking at the opening of a new cemetery at Westgate Hill. Pengilly stated that he had had 'many opportunities of painful observations on that subject' when trying to accommodate the remains of his friends at Ballast Hills. The packed burial ground could not cope with the demand for burials and it was hoped that the new cemetery at Westgate Hill would solve many of these problems.

Westgate Hill also had extra protection to thwart bodysnatchers, with 12ft high walls and deeper graves introduced at the site. Yet, a brief article appearing in the *Newcastle Courant* showed that the local parishioners wanted something more than just bodysnatching deterrents. A list of eight views expressed by the committee and subscribers of the new cemetery was published and at the top of the list was the request for 'a burial place so large and capacious, that the necessity of prematurely breaking the ground and disturbing the remains of the deceased should no longer exist.'

Overcrowding within churchyards in England and Scotland was then wide-spread, as was a disregard for how the corpses of the poorer members of the parish were treated. Stories of sextons keeping pauper graves open until they were full and only then covering the grave with a thin layer of soil, often appeared in the press. The poor bore the brunt of the lax burial practices of some parishes.

The *Morning Chronicle* printed an article in 1778 highlighting the depraved state of London churchyards:

> 'One of the great sources of putrid disorders, in this metropolis, is the little attention paid to the interment of the poor. In some burial grounds, near the centre of this city, the graves, or pits, for the reception of the lower sort of people, are made sufficiently wide to contain four, five or six wooden coffins abreast, and deep enough to hold twice as many in depth: these pits, after each burial, are covered with a few loose boards and a little mould [soil] to keep the coffin from common view.'

Similarly, Dumbarton kirkyard in the west of Scotland became so overcrowded that in order to find space for the next interment, a metal rod would be pushed into the soil and a record made of how far down it could go. In 'God's Acres of Dumbarton' (1888), Donald MacLeod commented that 'the living, as a rule, would persist in burying the dead in the old kirkyard, although it was quite too full.'

By the first half of the nineteenth century graveyards were being targeted more frequently. This coincided with the rise in private anatomy schools and the number of students studying medicine – a reported 520 at London's private anatomy schools alone in 1820. The report of the 1828 Select Committee on Anatomy, stated that 'although students now attending the schools of Anatomy in London exceed 800, not more than 500 of this number actually dissect'. Even so, the meagre supply legitimately available from the gallows was woefully inadequate for this amount of medical students.

Rapacious bodysnatchers were eager to take advantage of the situation and the need to protect the dead was becoming paramount for parishes throughout the country. The *Oxford Journal* reported as early as 1759, that 'this monstrous practice is now become so common that it is hoped the legislature will think it necessary to interpose'. But the authorities did not take action, and instead the duty of protecting the sepulchres of the dead fell to their loved ones and fellow members of the local parish.

In December 1819 the *Norfolk Telegraph* stated that 'the burial grounds in London and its neighbourhood are at this time carefully guarded, that the res-urrection men are prevented from following their avocation.' Parishioners were taking action themselves, ensuring that if bodies were needed for the dissection table then they would be acquired from some other, less well-protected parish.

Deciding how best to protect the body of a loved one from the grasping hands of the anatomists boiled down to two main factors: the geographical area and money. Even the richer members of society were at risk of being snatched. Although they fared a little better than those among the lower levels, the wealthy were not impervious to the skills of the resurrectionist. Professional bodysnatchers were starting to emerge, leaving behind opportunists and students.

The most successful were cunning individuals who could enter a churchyard, exhume a corpse and ship their wares to a medical school before the public even realised the churchyard had been violated. If the process was carried out discreetly and without too much disturbance a busy churchyard could keep a resurrectionist in work for months.

Advice for grieving families regularly appeared in newspapers whenever an incident of bodysnatching was discovered and ranged from the mundane to the outrageous. One easy and often effective deterrent was to dig deeper graves – advice taken on board by the sextons of Speen, Berkshire, whenever they carried out burials within the parish. Yet, this occasionally caused problems too, as an incident reported in 1822 by *The Examiner* demonstrates. In his enthusiasm to deter the bodysnatchers, a gravedigger from Anderston, Glasgow, was buried alive in the deep grave he had dug and had to be rescued by some weavers who happened to be passing by.

Some homemade prevention methods bordered on the outrageous, such as the precautions taken by one landowner in February 1824, after bodysnatchers had targeted a remote parish in Northumberland. According to the *Carlisle Journal*:

> 'to prevent such depredations in future . . . graves [should] be made shorter than the coffin, and be excavated at the bottom, so as to admit the head under solid ground. It is then impossible to raise it by the feet, and the ground must be cut away above the head.'

In addition to burying the head in 'solid ground', the landowner went one step further and introduced to the coffin 'a mixture of percussion powder and gunpowder be placed on a wire inside of the coffin, to explode on its being opened . . . this will retain its explosive power for one month, in which time the corpse will generally be unfit for dissection.'

This rather final solution was taken a stage further by a Dundee father when he buried his young child in 1823. Fearing that the resurrection men would take his child's corpse for the dissecting table, he had placed a small box 'containing dreadful apparatus' inside the coffin, which was connected to a series of four wires and subsequently secured to the coffin lid. The device was rigged so that as soon as the coffin lid was tampered with, the resurrectionist would 'be blown up' by the gunpowder placed within the box.

One York newspaper even suggested pouring sulphuric acid over each corpse prior to burial, in order to render them useless for dissection. In 1815, when John Warrington was executed for robbery at Symington Toll, Scotland, his friends poured vitriol and quicklime into his coffin to ensure his corpse would be useless for the surgeons.

Not all homemade deterrents were as destructive. The poor were the most vulnerable members of the parish in death as in life, especially those buried in a paupers' grave, which provided notoriously rich pickings for the bodysnatcher. Some had the heart-warming notion that by placing a token of some sort on top of the grave, like a pebble or a twig, they would be able to detect any signs that a grave had been violated.

In 1824 a white stone was placed on top of a grave in Scoonie, Fife, although it is not known if this was left by loved ones to indicate if the grave had been tampered with or placed by resurrection men hoping to secure a cadaver later that evening. Unfortunately, this simple detection device was also an excellent indicator of a fresh burial. All freshly filled graves had a few identifying marks – loose soil, possibly raised in a 'hump', perhaps a few fresh flowers, not to mention the token that the grieving relatives had laid on top of the grave – all aiding the grave robber to identify when and where a fresh cadaver was available.

Reconnaissance missions carried out by the bodysnatcher close to the day of the funeral, would be used to spot these tokens. They might have already made a mental note of where the grave was after having attended the funeral in person, pretending to be a grieving relative. Some bodysnatchers would even make sketches of the location and the layout of, for instance, a bundle of sticks seemingly placed at random on top of the grave. When visiting the graveside later that evening, it was but a case of removing the token, exhuming the body and replacing the token in the exact same position as before. Simple, and very effective.

The most basic ideas were often perhaps the best in protecting graveyards. Another common practice was mixing either straw or stones in with the soil when back-filling the grave. This easy cost-effective deterrent is described in *Berrow's Worcester Journal* in 1822, having originally appeared in *Medicina Clerica* a publication designed to give 'hints to the clergy for the healthful and comfortable discharge of their ministerial duties':

Correct Account of
THE RIOTS

Concerning Stealing Dead Bodies, in different parts of Glasgow,
On saturday and Sunday, the 1st and 2d March, 1823; with an account of
the Dead Bodies, and the Heads Limbs & pieces of Human Bodies Found.

Early on Friday night. the neighbourhood of the College
Church-yard, was alarmed by noises proceeding from the church
yard, when the watchman on that station sprung his rattle, and
having procured assistance, they entered the 'grave-yard, where
they found three doctors and a boy, whom they escorted to the
Police Office.

In the middle of the above night, the watchman at Lady-well
street remarked two well-dressed persons hastening toward the
High Church-yard An interval of some minutes elapsed, when
he perceived the same persons return, followed by some others
bearing something tied up in a large bundle.—An alarm was
instantly given, when the watchmen assembled, and having secured the man who was bearing the bundle, and a young man
who appeared of the same party, they then proceeded to examine
the bundle; which was found to be the body of a man deceased,
who had lived in the Havannah, and who was lately interred in
the aforesaid church yard. The fellow that carried the corpse
made such opposition to his being taken, by striking. kicking, and
biting the watchmen, that they thought proper to bind him and the
corpse together, on a hurley, when they were removed to the Office. It was with great difficulty the police could prevent the
crowd that assembled from taking vengeance on him. The son of
the man disinterred, appeared at the Office some time afterwards,
to claim his father's body.

Drawing conclusions from those and other events, it was that a great concourse
of people assembled opposite a lecture room in Duke street, on Saturday
morning, at half past nine o' clock, when they proceeded to break open the
door, when a most appalling scene presented itself... On the floor, stood a large
tub, in which was found a number of heads, arms and legs. On the table lay
the whole body of a woman with long hair. The body of a man lay aside it,
with the head cut off, and the entrails out, and otherwise dissected. At the
end of the room was a complete skeleton. Other mangled bodies were found,
and limbs and mutilated fragments of bodies were strewed about the room. The
mob were so exasperated that, siezing the bodies and every thing found in the
room, they tossed them into the streets. They were proceeding to demolish
the premises until the arrival of Bailie Snell, with the Police, and a detachment
of soldiers, when a proper guard was stationed to prevent farther violence.

Yesterday forenoon, a crowd assembled in Portland street, at another lecture
room, when they had proceeded to break the outer door, and were proceeding
to the room, when they were alarmed by the arrival of the Police. Some bones
were found on the premises, and were tossed about by the crowd. Guards are
placed to prevent mischief while a legal investigation is going on, to satisfy the
public mind.

Another case of bodysnatching highlighted in 1823 in the frequently targeted city of Glasgow.
(National Library of Scotland shelf mark: L.C. Fol. 73(046))

ROBBERY OF
Dead Bodies.

An account of that woman who died in Jamaica Street, Edinburgh, on the 3d Feb. 1825, and after being coffined and locked up, the room was entered by a window, the corpse stolen, and the coffin filled with stones; also the apprehension of a resurrection man in Haddington church-yard with the instruments employed for lifting the dead. Likewise an account of the discovery of the body of a man in a trunk, by a porter at Pettycur while carrying it to the steam-boat, on Tuesday the 8th Feb. and which had been brought from Dundee on its way to Edinburgh.

Those who follow the unlawful employment of stealing dead bodies are now contriving, in place of taking them out of their graves, to get possession of them before they are buried. Last week. a poor woman, who lived by herself, died in Jamaica Street, when her body was placed in a coffin and the house shut up. In the course of Thursday night the house was entered by a window from a back lane, the body was carried off, and the coffin filled with stones. The discovery was not made till Friday, when the interment was about to take place.

On Friday the 30th ult. about one o'clock, the watchmen, when going their rounds in the church-yard of Haddington, had their attention suddenly arrested by the sound of a whistle; being fully convinced of the sound having proceeded from a person intending to desturb the silent repositories of the dead, they stationed themselves near to the place where four bodies were lately interred, to wait in silence the approach of the resurrectionist. In a few minutes he leaped over the wall, carrying along with him a bag, a rope, and a screw, (such as is used on similiar occasions), when he was immediately laid hold of by Andrew Kerse, late of the 49th regiment, who, with the assistance of his neighbour watchmen, conducted him to the watch-house, in the coal-honse of which he was confined till eight o'clock, when he was carried before Provost Dodds for examination; but he persisted in silence in his presence, as he had hitherto done in the watch-house; he was therefore committed to jail for farther examination. He appears to be an Irishman, but refuses to give his name or the number of his accomplices.

An occurrence happened at Pettycur on Tuesday forenoon, which nearly proved fatal to the person concerned. The Coach arrived from Dundee with passengers and luggage for the Steam Boat at Pettycur for Leith; the porters employed carrying a trunk from the Coach to to the Boat, thought that a nauseous smell peoceeded from it and immediately threw it down, waiting for their employer, who was well known as a constant weekly passenger for some time past; and when he came forward, the crowd which by this time began to get numerous, demanded to see it opened, which he stiffly refused, untill he saw that violence was going to be applied, when he told them that his master was in the Inn, and he would go and get the key. Judging his intention, they watched him, to see if he would enter the Inn, but as soon as he passed the door he took to his heels, and endeavoured to make his escape; he was however overtaken, and was with great difficulty lodged in Kingborn Jail, not without some cuts and bruises from the usage of the crowd; who, especially the women, manifested a determination to give him summary punishment; the trunk was opened, and the body of a dead man found therein, supposed to be taken from [some of the Church-yards in Dundee.

Edinburgh, Printed for J. Sellen

Edinburgh being the target in 1825, this broadside shows the lengths to which some bodysnatchers would go to obtain a cadaver for the anatomists.

An unusual double entry in the criminal registers for 1833 showing two pairs of bodysnatchers and the 'notorious Mrs Sutton'.

(HO 27/46 (407) Reproduced with kind permission of The National Archives)

RESURRECTION MEN.

THESE Pests of Society, whose Operations disturb the Repose of many a Village, and add Bitterness to the Mourner's Sorrow, have lately given an Example of Dexterity in their Calling, such as we never before heard of. Not satisfied with robbing the Grave of its solid Contents, and desecrating the hallowed Rites of the Tomb, they have now shewn their Power in raising disembodied *Spirits*, and have been seen to exhibit the Phantasma in various Parts of the County of Northumberland.—We refer to a Funeral that took place lately in the Town of Alnwick, which was most numerously attended; when, with much Solemnity of Manner and great funereal Pomp, a certain "Spirit of Acrimony"—and certain "Feelings of Animosity" were deposited in the Tomb of "everlasting Oblivion," that had been carefully prepared for their Reception by a respectable Grave-digger, called Thomas Little.—But scarcely had the sorrowing Multitude dispersed—nor yet had that Sun sunk in the western Wave, which was so eloquently invoked to penetrate the Bosom from which these defunct Feelings had been exorcised, and bear Testimony to the Purity that pervaded its inmost Recesses, when it was discovered, that impious Hands had invaded the sacred Regions of their Tomb—had burst the Cerements in which they were enshrined, and given them again to exercise their baleful Influence amongst the Inhabitants of this upper Earth. They were partially seen on the Road from Alnwick to Newcastle, on the very Day of their Interment, but have since been publicly exhibited in Shields, strewing the "Flowers of Rhetoric" in its Streets—assisting "Fancy to spread her painted Wings, and display her glowing Colours"—and teaching the industrious Inhabitants of that Town, the important Lesson, that, however they may manage Matters with the Sea that lashes their Shores, they cannot get up to the "Moon to turn her Course," or "scatter, from their fixed and immutable Orbits, the wide rolling Planets of Heaven," in allusion, it is supposed, to some Irish Stars that stand stock still all the Time they are moving. It is thought that the decent Ceremony of Burial had better be abandoned in Future, as it is clear, that nothing now is safe from the Ingenuity and Audacity of these vile Resurrectionists.

Reprinted by M. Barker, Hexham.

The wording on this notice showed how despised and disgusted the populace were in the North of England at the increasing resourcefulness of Britain's bodysnatchers.

(ZMD 02-19 Reproduced with permission of Northumberland Archives)

Stored safely behind a locked gate, the two halve[s] Old Alloway mortsafe, Ayrshire are a grim remin[der] bodysnatching in the area. (Author's own image)

The watch-house at Old Pentland, Midlothian marks the site of the first recorded case of bodysnatching in Scotland. In 1742 John Samuel stole the body of Gaston Johnson from his grave.

A fine example of a watch-house can be found in Symington, South Lanarkshire where the small windows are directed over the open fields beyond and into the churchyard. (Author's own image)

The striking watchtower at Dalkeith, Midlothian was built at a cost of £150 in 1827. (Author's own image)

'Resurrection Business has been going on here of late'. Detail in a letter dated 25 March 182[?] showing precautions taken against the bodysnatchers in the North East of England.

The unusual mortsafe at Luss, Argyll & Bute hopefully keeps a cadaver safe behind its encasement.
(Author's own image)

Perth Burying Ground Protecting Association 'A call to Arms' for men of Perth parish, Perthshire. (By courtesy of Perth & Kinross Council Archive Collection Ref: PE47/119)

The Perth Burying Ground
PROTECTING ASSOCIATION.

Mr.

You have been balloted along with   others, to Watch the *Grey-friars' Burying Ground*, on the night of   first,—The Watch will assemble at the Burying Ground Watch-house, at   o'clock evening precisely. Strict punctuality is expected.

By the LAWS of the ASSOCIATION, a Member who finds it inconvenient to give his personal attendance on the Watch, may, in his place, send one of his Family, (if above Sixteen years of age,) or one of his Shopmen, or Clerks, or Journeymen, or a Substitute belonging to the Association, and approved of by the Committee. The Committee will provide a Balloted Substitute if you give the Officer notice to that effect, and pay him

☞ You will please inform the Officer whether you will Watch personally or how?

WILLIAM GREIG, Secretary.

PERTH,   185
Please bring this Ticket with you.

J. Crerar, Printer, Perth.

The iron rods attached to the Kilmaurs mortsafe, Ayrshire can be seen poking out from beneath the grass, keeping safe the cadaver of the final occupant.

Ramshorn Kirkyard, Glasgow. The prerogative of wealthy; the caged lair. Even these impressive fortresses failed to stop the bodysnatchers in their tracks. (Author's own image)

Evidence from the trial of John Barker and John Beaumont at the January Sessions for the West Riding of Yorkshire, 1827. (West Yorkshire Archive Service, Kirklees, KC165/42 (part))

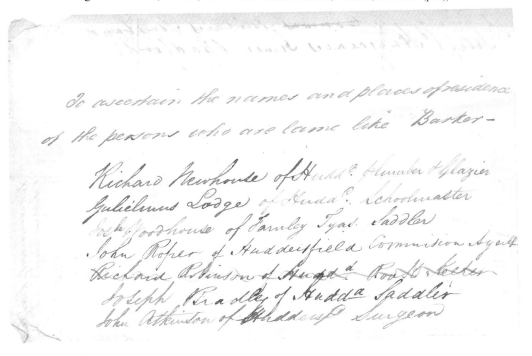

Much distress was caused to the residents of Barnsley, South Yorkshire when William Yeardley descended on the quiet parish to rob the graves in 1829.

(Sheffield Archives and Local Studies Library Picture Sheffield Collection reference number arc01045)

BODY-STEALING,
AT BARNSLEY.

On Tuesday last, February 3rd, 1829, the town of Barnsley was thrown into a state of considerable excitement, by the apprehension of a man and woman charged with the odious offence of body-stealing. The man had for some weeks been noticed walking about the town without any employment or visible means of subsistence, and on this day was observed taking a box to the coach-office, addressed to "Mary Jones, No. 1, Prince's-street, Edinbro'." The constable followed, and suspecting all was not right, insisted on opening the box. The man at first refused to allow him, but finding the officer determined, he said, "Do not open it here; it contains what you expect to find, open it before the Magistrates. He was instantly lodged in "durance vile," and the female who had resided with him as wife or companion, was also taken into custody. The box, on being opened, appeared to be filled with hay, but on removing the latter, a male child, about two years of age, was found at the bottom, without a particle of linen upon it. Its little legs had been contracted so as to prevent the body moving about in the box. It was evident the child had died a natural death, about two or three days before, but nothing transpired to shew the manner in which the body had been obtained. The prisoners were brought before the Rev. Dr. Corbett, and Joseph Beckett, Esq. on Wednesday, and were fully committed to take their trials at the ensuing Pontefract Sessions. On removing the prisoners to their cells, the feelings of the populace were so much excited, that it was with difficulty the officers could protect them from their indignation. No person came forward to identify the child, and it was the opinion of the Magistrates, that it been taken from the neighbourhood of Sheffield. The man declined answering ... y questions as to the manner, or from whence he obtained it; but from the evidence of Samuel Howarth, at whose house the prisoner lodged, it is probable that the child came from Sheffield or the neighbourhood, as a man brought the prisoner a basket the night before from this town. A man, who is a weaver in Barnsley, buried a child ten days ago, about four years old; he has examined the grave, but the child is gone: and it is stated by Howarth, that on the night of the funeral, the prisoner and his wife were out till midnight, and the next day a parcel was forwarded to Edinburgh. A regular set of implements was found at the prisoners' lodgings for opening graves and wrenching coffins. They were both committed to take their trials at the Sessions, and an inquest was directed to be held over the child.

The child thus discovered has flaxen coloured hair, with a ringworm on the left side of the head, about the size of half-a-crown, with the hair cut off.—William Yeardley, who is now in custody at Sheffield, states, that he brought the child away from Sheffield in a hamper on Sunday morning the 1st inst.

We understand that one of the accomplices was apprehended on Friday night last; it appears he left Barnsley about ten days ago, on the coach with a hamper and a box, which are supposed to contain two dead bodies, directed for the said "Mary Jones, of Edinbro'." He returned to Barnsley on Friday afternoon, and enquired for his friend, who was in custody. The person who he enquired of sending for the constable, he was also immediately apprehended. They are supposed to be the same gang that has infested Sheffield and its neighbourhood. We regret to state, that the Church-yards of Barnsley has been plundered of their dead to a great extent.

T. ORTON, PRINTER, SHEFFIELD.

Photo of 'Resurrection Cottage'. The supposed home of bodysnatcher John Craig Hodgson.

(West Yorkshire Archive Service, Sheepscar, 2004713_3907412)

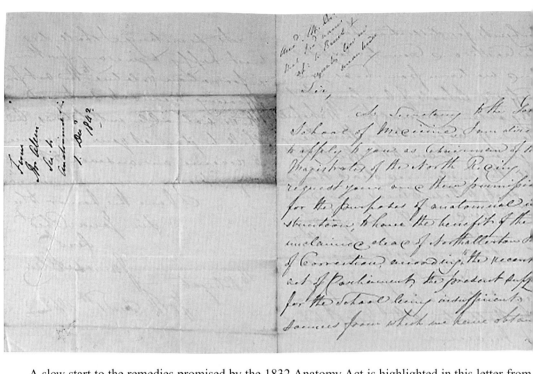

A slow start to the remedies promised by the 1832 Anatomy Act is highlighted in this letter from the York School of Medicine to the Northallerton House of Correction, North Yorkshire requesting the bodies of the 'unclaimed dead' according to the Act.

(Reproduced with kind permission of North Yorkshire County Record Office QSB 1843 1-17 Letter 1 Dec 1842)

Subjects for dissertation have been the Castle and County Hospital. And we hear from Leeds and Sheffield Schools of Anatomy that they obtain several from Wakefield House of Correction, there being a general Order to the effect that all the unclaimed dead should be sent to these places according to their use. Therefore finding our supplies inadequate, the Teachers respectfully solicit your consent and your fellow Magistrates to a like grant from Northallerton to the York School of Medicine

As Secretary I shall be most happy to give any further information relative to the act for affording means to sustain these valuable institutions. I shall be glad at your convenience to receive an answer to this request.

I have the honor to be Sir Your Obed serv

James Allen

16 Petergate

York Dec 1st 1842

'As soon as the corpse is deposited let a truss of long wheaten straw be opened, and deposited in the grave in layers, as equally as may be, with every layer of earth, till the whole is filled up. By this method the corpse will be effectively secured, as may be found by experience, for it is certain, that the longest night will not afford time sufficient to empty the grave, though all common implements of grave digging be made use of for the abominable purpose.'

The idea was to make digging as difficult as possible and in essence, put the bodysnatcher off before they had reached the coffin.

Thomas (or in some accounts Ralph) Heesom decided to use straw as a deterrent when he buried his daughter Hannah on New Year's Eve 1828. Prior to Hannah's burial, Heesom sent a bundle of straw to the sexton of St Mary's Church in Whitkirk, on the outskirts of Leeds, with the intention that it might be placed in alternate layers between the soil when the grave was filled up. However, the sexton, either not understanding Heesom's wishes or aiming to make the work of the resurrection men easier, placed all of the straw in one bundle across the top of the coffin lid.

When Thomas Brown, a brick-maker by trade and a lone bodysnatcher, stole Hannah's body less than twenty-four hours after it had been interred, the bundle of straw on the coffin lid and the unusually shallow grave provided no deterrent. Brown, however, was an amateur bodysnatcher and he left a trail of evidence in his wake. After three attempts to remove Hannah's coffin from the ground, being disturbed each time by passers-by, Brown also had considerable difficulty in removing the coffin lid.

Eventually, after what appears to have been quite a struggle, Brown removed Hannah's body 'out of the coffin and tied it up in his shirt . . . put it into a handkerchief and took it direct to a surgery'. Hannah was only five years of age and had died from hydrocephalus (water on the brain).

Hannah's coffin and her burial clothes were discovered in a nearby field by her mother soon after. Brown's inexperience was not well received by other resurrection men in the area. Seasoned bodysnatcher William Yeardley was the principal witness at Brown's trial. Having alerted Mr Heesom to the fate of his daughter and received the ten-pound reward for doing so, Yeardley quite openly stated that: 'Brown had performed his work so badly, it would prevent them [bodysnatchers] from doing anything in that way, in that neighbourhood, for a year.'

Why was Yeardley giving evidence to implicate a fellow bodysnatcher? It seems that Brown and Yeardley had received an order for a cadaver, 'a small one, either male or female', from two surgeon apprentices in Leeds. When Yeardley was certain Brown had delivered the body, he informed Mr Heesom of the terrible deed and also accompanied the police to Hull, where Brown was eventually arrested.

It is unclear exactly why Yeardley turned Brown in, although there are a few possibilities. Perhaps Yeardley was giving up Brown in order not to be imprisoned himself or his action could have been part of a larger plan? The ten-pound reward and the two pounds seven shillings received for Hannah's body was certainly more than the two men could have earned in a year through honest work.

Mixing straw or stones into the soil when backfilling a grave did not always prove to be effective. In 1825, John Williams, Thomas Mills and Margaret Lansdowne, were indicted for stealing a body from Northolt Churchyard in the parish of Greenford, Middlesex. The body was highly sought after, for the deceased had been suffering from a disease in the head which had long baffled surgeons.

During the burial, the soil was returned to an extra deep grave, with straw and large stones mixed in as it was filled. Yet, as the *Morning Chronicle* pointed, out, these precautions were useless, for the body was seen being taken out of a dung heap one week later. Williams and Mills were both sentenced to six months and one month's imprisonment respectively, whilst Lansdowne was found not guilty.

Preventative measures involved additions to the churchyard, as well as embellishments to individual graves. A number of parishes embraced the idea of increasing the height of the churchyard wall. Just as the theory behind digging deep graves was quite straightforward: burying a coffin deep meant it would take the bodysnatcher longer to reach the lid. Similarly, building a high wall would take longer for them to scale. Walls were scaled on a regular basis though, and ladders could easily be stolen when required.

A small article appeared in the *Morning Post* in November, 1822 giving an account of William Hodges, who was tried at Lambeth Street Magistrates Court for attempting to steal bodies from Poplar Chapel burial ground. Hodges stated that he was approached by two men as he was passing along Brick Lane. They asked if he was out of work and, if so, whether he would like to earn himself a crown. Hodges, after agreeing, found himself being propelled over the wall of the burial ground, because he was the lightest man in the party.

The *Morning Chronicle* reported on the witness statement given by Coleman, the parish constable. On returning to the churchyard after apprehending Hodges, Coleman, together with Joseph Piper, a parish watchman, surveyed the scene in front of them. The usual bodysnatching implements were found: bag, shovel and sack, not to mention a scaling ladder and an 'iron instrument for bursting open the coffins'. The items had been placed carefully along the top of the burial ground wall and a long sack was used to cover the glass protruding from the top of the wall.

But how did Hodges come to know about the burial of the two individuals he had tried to snatch? Hodges had been spotted regularly walking about the burial ground on Sundays after church services, inspecting graves and enquiring how old the deceased was and what they had died of, no doubt making a mental note of potential targets. That November night, Hodges had gone one step too far in his preliminary enquiries when one of the victims, a Mrs Patmore, was being buried on the 22 November, not only did Hodges ask the sexton if it was a 'parish job', but he also helped to fill in her grave.

It was well-known that a low wall around a churchyard offered no security against the 'sack 'em up men'. One night in 1818, a party of bodysnatchers entered the churchyard in Christchurch, Surrey. *The Times* noted that 'the wall by which the ground is surrounded is too low and defective for the purpose of security'. The bodysnatchers stole three adults and one child that night.

Church authorities had to attempt improvements to reassure parishioners. In the burial ground situated on Portugal Street in the parish of St Clement Danes in London, cast iron railings as well as a wrought iron gate were installed in 1820, to thwart the nocturnal activities of the local bodysnatchers. Meanwhile, in 1828, St Mary's Church in Hitchin installed iron railings around the churchyard, following the snatching of Elizabeth Whitehead's body. This simple prevention method was adopted by a number of parishes and high walls surrounding churchyards can still be seen today in many parishes throughout the country.

Alterations such as these were not considered suitable for all churchyards and instead, where funds allowed, parishes set up a watch on the graveyard following each interment. Settling in to watch over a grave for a few nights until the body had had time to decay was not a new idea and many parishioners took it upon themselves to watch over the graves of loved ones and friends.

In 1828, one man from Drypool, East Yorkshire reportedly watched over the grave of his friend for two weeks to ensure that he remained untouched by the resurrection men. Four years earlier, a man watching over the grave of his recently interred wife apparently disturbed two bodysnatchers, who were attempting to steal her body from the parish church at Grinstead.

In Wakefield, West Yorkshire, the parish church was targeted so heavily that the watch made checks on the grave of the recently interred Tommy Baldwin, a flock dresser from Quebec Street, 'seven or eight times a night and a mark made on it could tell whether it had been touched'. On another occasion, the grave of a local wine merchant Mr Wells was watched for nearly six weeks, at a cost of 'five shillings and some whiskey each evening' which was no doubt graciously received by the watch.

Some parishes provided a purpose-built structure in the form of a watch-house or watchtower for the men to occupy during their graveyard shift. The structure would consist of anything from an elaborate hexagonal tower, such as the examples seen at Banchory-Ternan in Aberdeenshire or High Bradfield in South Yorkshire. More commonly, a basic structure comprised merely a door, window and rudimentary fireplace, such as that found in Old Pentland, Midlothian or the remains of the watch-house at Whitsome, Berwickshire.

Examples of surviving structures, although predominant in Scotland, still pepper churchyards throughout England. London boasts a number of watch-houses, including examples at Rotherhithe, Bermondsey and Wanstead. There are two fine examples at Warblington in Hampshire, where, although no recorded cases of bodysnatching have been found to date, the threat was evidently considered sufficient for these two structures to be commissioned in 1828.

Watch-towers and houses are typically found in a far corner of the churchyard or built into the churchyard wall. They were placed there to provide the watch with uninterrupted views across the churchyard and the surrounding neighbour-hood. Windows would be positioned facing the most obvious entrance to the churchyard, so that the watch could observe the bodysnatcher in action. Some parishes provided protection from the elements by utilising pre-existing struc-tures, such as a 'bathing machine'. This was similar in style to the Victorian bathing huts wheeled to the water's edge and it was reputedly in use at Florence Place, the oldest Jewish Cemetery in Brighton, Sussex.

The watchmen housed within these towers were usually either employed by the parish or had volunteered to keep guard over the recently dug graves of members of their congregation. A document from one Northumberland church, the 'Rules Respecting the Watch in Doddington Churchyard', gives an idea of what a typical night on 'watch' would be like. Of the sixteen rules in total, two in particular offer the best example of a watchman's duties:

'Rule 10 – That the watchmen are to be supplied with coal, candles, gunpowder and shot, at the expense of the Society and discretion of the Clerk and Committee. . .

'Rule 13 – That the watch must be on duty between twilight and daylight, summer and winter, after the interment of each Corpse so long as shall be deemed necessary by the Committee.'

Doddington's watch-house was built in 1826, possibly in reaction to a body-snatching incident less than thirty miles away in Edrom, Berwickshire. On 10 November 1825, two men who reportedly had the appearance of bodysnatchers were driving a gig from Hardens to Longformacus. When stopped by suspicious locals who wanted to examine the contents of the gig, the men escaped across the moors. Sure enough a body was found hidden in the gig, that of local man Peter McGall, (or Mackall) who had been buried in Edrom nine days earlier.

Failure to watch a grave and therefore having to retrieve a corpse after it had been snatched could be a costly affair. The churchwardens of West Huntspill, Somerset, found this out in a very early case of suspected bodysnatching in 1735. Entries made in the churchwardens' accounts, now lost but recounted in a contemporary edition of the *Western Mercury*, give details of payments made to the neighbouring parish of Bridgwater for the return of the body of Alice Hawkeswell. Alice's body was found naked after being taken from her grave, presumably by bodysnatchers. West Huntspill parish paid five shillings for a new shroud for Alice and a further one shilling and ten pence for a bag to carry her home in. Her body was also watched whilst it was waiting to be returned, at a total cost of ten shillings.

Grave clubs or watch clubs were formed in many parishes throughout England. Rothwell, near Leeds, established one after being visited by bodysnatchers in 1827, who also targeted the nearby parishes of Sandal Magna, Alverthorpe and Wakefield. In Swinton, Manchester a 'watchers club' was established in the Bulls Head public house, opposite the graveyard of St Peter's. Subscriptions would be paid on a weekly basis and, when any member needed the grave of a loved one watched, the men of the club would rally round and keep a vigil over the graveyard.

What happened if the men watching the graveyard spotted a bodysnatcher at work? Many of those undertaking surveillance duties would have been doing so out of good neighbourly feeling and would have reacted instinctively when faced with a potentially dangerous situation. In 1822, a suspicious bodysnatching case appeared in the *Morning Post*. Two men had been discovered lying in a grave in the churchyard of East Grinstead, after they had both been shot in the legs.

The men claimed that they had been 'induced by some London resurrection men' to disinter a recently buried corpse, but they had been discovered in the act and subsequently shot by the watch. Bodysnatchers were also fired upon in the Midlothian parish of Newton, where bullet marks can still be seen on a gravestone in the churchyard.

Remote churchyards, as well as those in highly populated cities were also targeted by bodysnatchers. Here, any additional shelter from the elements would have gone far to help ensure that the parish received a higher grade of surveillance from its watchmen, especially if a fire could be lit and a warm drink made. The exposed site at High Bradfield in South Yorkshire is a perfect example. The biting winter wind blows viciously up the valley, hitting the churchyard head on. The isolation of this site might have provided a little extra time for 'snatching', as not even the keenest watchman would have wanted to be exposed to the elements here for very long.

The much photographed watchtower built at High Bradfield in the late eighteenth century is believed to be the only surviving example of a watchtower in Yorkshire. Although it was intended to house those keeping watch on the churchyard, it did not play any part in the detection of the bodysnatcher Joseph Hall in the early hours of 6 February 1830. The gig Hall had procured was spotted not far from the churchyard and, suspecting it was parked there for nefarious purposes, three local men, Charles Greaves, James Morton and John Morton, entered the churchyard to investigate further.

Hall was found standing in the grave of the recently buried Joseph Fox, digging soil out of it. Hall overheard Greaves and the two Mortons talking and immediately leapt out of Fox's grave, trying to make his escape. He did not get far, and was apprehended sixty yards from the grave itself. Whilst in custody, it transpired that the audacious Hall had been seen at the interment of Fox's body, standing by his graveside at the funeral service. Perhaps it was during this reconnaissance that he noticed that owing to a large stone causing an obstruction, Joseph Fox's grave was unusually shallow – less than 4ft deep. Hall's case was duly heard at the Pontefract sessions and, after much deliberation, the jury returned a verdict of guilty, and Hall was sentenced to six months' imprisonment.

Today, many surviving watch-houses are used to store gardening equipment necessary for the upkeep of the graveyard, such as at Cromdale in the Scottish Highlands or Hamilton, South Lanarkshire. Others have been converted into private residences, like High Bradfield and the watch-house at St Cuthbert's Churchyard, Edinburgh. Equal numbers of watch-houses have been left to erode, such as Whitsome in the Borders; swamped under a march of ivy or the deteriorated example tucked away in St Mary's Churchyard in Morpeth, Tyneside.

Just because relatives or the parish had secured men to watch over the churchyard or provided a watch-house to shelter them did not guarantee that all newly-dug graves would remain undisturbed. In 1817, Thomas Duffin (some reports call him William) and William Marshall (also recorded as John) were indicted for assaulting John Sharpe at St Mary's Church, Lambeth when trying to steal a body. Sharpe had employed Duffin and Marshall (the former a gravedigger, the latter his assistant) to watch over the recently interred 'against the depredations of persons engaged in the unpopular occupation for securing subjects for the hospitals'. Such was the level of corpse-theft from St Mary's that man-traps were also set to help protect the dead from the living.

Since Duffin and Marshall had been employed 'scarcely a night passed without a body being stolen' and, suspecting the pair were not what they seemed, Sharpe, together with the sexton John Segars decided to keep a watch over the churchyard themselves. That night five freshly dug graves were filled with recently deceased parishioners – a prime target for resurrection men. Having arranged an alternative watch made up of men from the parish, Sharpe joined them in the churchyard and waited to confirm his suspicions.

Around midnight, movement was heard as the man traps laid were disarmed by Duffin and Marshall and the sound of a spade hitting a coffin was soon detected. Sharpe and his men confronted the two bodysnatchers and a struggle ensured, during which Sharpe received several blows with a sabre. Duffin and Marshall subsequently received two-year prison sentences for their assault on Sharpe. This was rather more severe than the usual fine or shorter sentence for the lesser crime of stealing a cadaver.

Duffin and Marshall were by no means the only corrupt watchmen to get involved in a bodysnatching scheme. Not surprisingly, some parishioners felt that they would watch the bodies of their loved ones more effectively than any hired watch ever could.

Corrupting the parish watch or sextons, working undercover as a gravedigger or even as a member of the watch party itself were all tactics used by the resurrectionists in a bid to provide easier access to any available cadavers. George Topping had been employed to watch St Pancras burial ground, but he was sentenced to three months' imprisonment in 1822 after his dealings with resurrection men came to light. Similarly, in November of the same year, John Hill, gravedigger at Crawford Private Burial Ground, Ewer Street, Southwark, was detained for 'aiding and abetting' 'body stealers' George Harris and Thomas Wallis after they had been found in the burial ground.

But not all watch-men could be bribed. On a cold January night in 1829, the watchmen of St George's Parish, Middlesex, King and Briggs, enjoyed a drink with bodysnatchers John North and William Parrott, who expounded upon the virtues of selling human bodies. North was adamant that he wanted no less than fourteen cadavers that same night, and he informed the watchmen that this would secure each of them five pounds for each cadaver lifted. Agreeing to meet in the churchyard between 1am and 2am the following morning, King and Briggs had in fact duped North and Parrott. They had already alerted the parish officials, who were lying in wait for the bodysnatchers to start their work.

After scaling a 14ft high wall topped with a *cheval de frise* – an additional defence made up of iron spikes set into the top of a wall – North and Parrott, together with two unidentified assistants, started digging for their haul. The first graves they opened did not prove fruitful, so they proceeded to work their way through the churchyard, opening several graves, before a signal was given by the watchmen to act. During his trial, North complained that he had been 'ill-used by the mob' when arrested, not to mention the fact that he had already been held for a period of five weeks. This failed to engage the sympathies of the presiding judge, however, who sentenced the pair to nine months' imprisonment with hard labour.

It was not always necessary to have a number of men stationed in a purpose-built tower to provide sufficient surveillance over a graveyard. In March 1833, two women whose bedroom overlooked the burial ground of the parish church in Rochdale, observed four resurrectionists at their work in the early hours one morning. They were too scared to raise the alarm on this occasion, so the bodysnatchers remained undisturbed, despite parish watchmen walking past the graveyard a number of times on their nightly rounds.

There was an altogether different outcome in 1849, when the faithful groom of a Mr Brown of Reedham, Norfolk, stood watch over his former master's grave and observed two resurrection men attempting to remove the cadaver. Armed with a double-barrelled gun, Brown shouted out to the bodysnatchers that he was armed. Shots were exchanged and one of the bodysnatchers clutched his chest, suggesting that he had been hit. Fearing that he would be the target of the next shot, the groom made haste to get help. Upon his return, the only trace of the injured resurrection man was a trail of blood leading through the churchyard.

If the bodysnatchers were successful in entering a churchyard that was overlooked by houses or in the vicinity of a particularly nosy neighbourhood, they would try to stop the inhabitants of houses that overlooked graveyards from noticing them at work. Dr Harper's chapel, located on Old Kent Road, London was overlooked by a number of houses, the inhabitants of which had already alerted the parish constable of the 'scenes which passed there during the night'. In order to prevent further observations, bodysnatchers targeting the chapel in 1818 placed 'boards and large pieces of timber against the windows to obscure the householders' view.

Although less corruptible, a grieving relative or concerned parishioner watching a recently filled grave would not necessarily be any more effective than a watchman. In the parish churchyard of St John's, Bermondsey, in January 1832 a young man named Goodman had a strong feeling that the corpse of his deceased father had been stolen from his grave. Goodman had already incorporated certain well-known bodysnatcher deterrents during the interment. The grave of Good-man senior had been dug to a depth of ten feet and his son had dutifully kept watch over his grave for four consecutive nights, but somehow the resurrection men had still secured the corpse. It was never found, even after a search of the hospitals and dissecting-rooms in the vicinity.

Just like watchtowers and watch-houses, mortsafes were predominantly found in Scotland. Those that survived the scrap metal hunt of World War Two are still scattered in churchyards throughout the Scottish countryside, offering a grim reminder of how widespread bodysnatching once was. The most famous Scottish mortsafes are those found in Greyfriars Kirkyard, Edinburgh.

The mortsafe was an ingenious deterrent often crafted by the local blacksmith and examples can be found in a number of different shapes and sizes. Mortsafes consisted of an iron cage or frame, which was placed over the coffin and was intended to remain *in situ* until the corpse had decomposed enough to render it useless to the surgeon, typically after a number of weeks.

A mortsafe could also consist of an iron coffin placed over the more traditional wooden coffin, again until the body became too putrid for dissection. Examples of this style of mortsafe can be found in the National Museum of Scotland, which proudly displays an 1828 iron mortsafe from Airth, Falkirk, and another used at Aberfoyle, Stirling.

Parishes would often purchase one or two mortsafes and subsequently hire them out as required. One Glasgow mortsafe was hired out at a shilling a day. Some parishioners also bought their own mortsafes, which were designed to stay buried along with the coffin. These simple structures were much more basic in nature and were fixed permanently around the coffin, effectively locking the lid down so that it could not be opened without removing the iron bars first. A fine example, consisting of granite blocks at each end, with an iron framework in-between, can be seen at Kirkton of Tough, Aberdeenshire.

Putting a mortsafe in place either required several men or the use of purpose-built 'mortsafe tackle', essentially three rods linked together at the top with an iron ring. These rods would be placed through rings attached to the mortsafe, with two at the shoulder end and one at the foot. The iron cage would then be lowered into the ground, over the coffin and the only way for it to be removed would have been with the mortsafe tackle. The tackle used at Inverurie Kirkyard, Aberdeenshire was kept in the baker's shop, away from the hands of resurrectionists.

Examples of mortsafes do survive throughout England but are often of very different design to those north of the border. The parish church in Henham,

Essex, has an elaborate mortsafe covering a stone inscribed with the date 1853, some years after the threat of bodysnatching had dissipated.

The use of the parish mortsafe was however for some, an insufficient deterrent against the bodysnatchers, and a few nervous individuals went to extremes to protect their loved ones. In 1828, a gentleman named Dowling from one Exeter parish had such a fear that the bodysnatchers would steal the corpse of his recently deceased wife that he kept her body above ground for over six weeks, in order to ensure that the body was 'in such a state of decomposition as to be totally unfit for the use if the anatomists'.

When Mr Dowling was finally satisfied that his wife, who had died in childbed, was past the point of freshness, she was buried along with their dead infant in a leaden coffin. As an extra precaution however, the lead coffin was then enclosed in two wooden coffins before being confined to the ground.

Although we have no record of whether or not a burial carried out in 1822 at Middleton, Lancashire resulted in the corpse being laid to rest in a leaden coffin, reports suggest that a child's body was kept at home for six weeks, until 'decomposition had set in and [the body] was sufficiently advanced' to be of any use to the medical profession. A cadaver that had been in the ground for even a week would have already started to show signs of decomposition. Discolouration and bloating would already be in process and the hair may have started to fall out, with the fingernails starting to shrink back into the skin.

These were factors that a seasoned resurrectionist would have been all too familiar with, but they would not render the body entirely useless for the surgeons. For a burial to be delayed for up to six weeks would have certainly ensured that the cadaver was beyond dissection, for not only would the teeth and nails have begun to fall out, but after this period of time, some sections of the cadaver may even have turned to liquid.

* * *

Parishes continued to guard against bodysnatchers for many years after the trade had subsided. Such was the concern that bodysnatchers would return to East Anstruther, Fife, that the East Anstruther Mortsafe Society only disbanded in 1869, some thirty-seven years after the passing of the Anatomy Act. The *Dundee Courier* commented that, as it was 'no longer necessary to secure the dead . . . and that the old members were fast dying out,' the decision had been taken 'to dissolve the society, to sell the safes and other property belonging to it, and divide the proceeds amongst the members'.

The Act had been introduced to quell the activities of the bodysnatchers and provide sufficient numbers of cadavers for teaching human anatomy. In reality, although the Act achieved these goals, they did not happen overnight and the fear that a loved one might still fall victim to the sack 'em up men, was still a reality in some parishes. In 1915, during digging at Aberlour, Speyside, a mortsafe was found still in situ. What is perhaps most surprising however, was the added discovery that the coffin locked within the mortsafe was empty.

A similar concept to the mortsafe, but far more ostentatious was the caged lair. Surviving examples can be seen in Ramshorn Kirkyard, Glasgow, as well as in Glasgow Cathedral and Edinburgh has a selection in Canongate Kirkyard. A caged lair was essentially an iron framework built around the site of burial, rather than encasing the coffin. The iron frames were either incorporated into stonework or free-standing structures, like the examples in Ramshorn Kirkyard. Often highly elaborate, caged lairs screamed wealth. In Greyfriars Kirkyard one site in particular stands out, that of surgeon William Inglis who was buried in 1792, obviously having had a great fear of ending up in the bodysnatcher's sack or on a colleague's dissecting table.

If you could afford neither a mortsafe nor a caged lair, you could resort to a 'resurrection stone', which was merely a large stone placed on top of the grave after burial. In order for it to be removed, a number of men would be needed, many more than would usually be in a gang of bodysnatchers. St Fittick's Kirkyard, Aberdeen was gifted a mortstone in 1816 and the 'Resurrection Stone' belonging to Pannal, North Yorkshire, was hired out at a guinea for two weeks and weighed over a ton. It can now been seen in the churchyard of St Robert's in Pannal. Lasswade's mortstone, in Midlothian also survives, as do examples at Logierait, Scotland, where the iron rings used to connect the stone to the mortsafe tackle can still be seen.

At the height of bodysnatching period, coffins made of iron or lead were introduced into graveyards throughout England, albeit with much furore. Their effectiveness surmounted any known prevention method to date, yet it failed to solve the resurrection problem.

In 1818 Edward Bridgman, a tallow chandler from London was in court defending his 'Patent Coffin'. The design was not in question – not at that time, anyway – but the longevity of the product. London churchyards were filling up rapidly, so how were they to accommodate coffins that would not rot, therefore permanently taking up valuable burial space? Bridgman's trial is widely documented in contemporary newspapers and centres on an interment in St Andrew, Holborn.

The Rector of St Andrew had refused to bury a Mrs Gilbert in one of Bridgman's coffins, causing her to remain unburied for several weeks. He had no issue with Mrs Gilbert being buried in the churchyard, but he would only accept her body if it was received in a more traditional wooden coffin. The problem, however, was that now Mrs Gilbert's corpse had been placed inside the iron coffin it could not be removed. The construction of the coffin ensured that it could not be reopened; fourteen spring catches engaged and locked the lid firmly in place once it was closed. Eventually the matter came to an end when the Consistory Court allowed iron coffins to be interred in churchyards and Mrs Gilbert could finally be laid to rest.

At the same time as Edward Bridgman was enthusing about his iron coffin, John Hughes was patenting a coffin in which the corpse was strapped down to a false bottom secreted inside a coffin. This used a similar concept to the coffin collar, where a metal collar or band was fastened to a piece of wood which was subsequently nailed to the bottom of the coffin. The iron collar would be fixed around the neck of the corpse, so that if the bodysnatchers did gain access to the coffin it could not be removed, no matter how hard the resurrectionist tugged.

In 1833, not even one year after the Anatomy Act was passed, evidence of this type of deterrent was discovered at the North West Burial Ground, Glasgow. A coffin was found fitted with 'two semicircles of iron, which had encompassed the neck and ancles (sic) of the corpse'. These had subsequently been screwed to the bottom of the coffin. A coffin collar, once in use at Kingskettle, Fife, can be seen at the National Museum of Scotland.

Finally, if neither well-guarded graves nor iron coffins deterred the body-snatcher, then perhaps this last preventive may have. 'More ingenious than lawful' was one way of describing the use of cemetery guns, and perhaps the most accurate, for the majority of these devices were simply regular poachers' guns 'rigged' and trained on graves instead of rabbit warrens.

Wires would be placed around the grave in the hope that when the body-snatcher brushed against one, he would trigger the gun mechanism. This idea however was to prove useless, for the resurrection men simply looked out for the wires and dismantled the apparatus before digging, only to train it over the mouth of the grave again when leaving. Occasionally, newspapers would report that a cemetery gun had been triggered in the dead of night, as the earlier case in Camden showed or that the unfortunate snatchers had got in the way of the bullet as was to be the case with the student bodysnatchers in Glasgow.

No amount of protection or delay in burial would stop a resurrectionist from getting hold of a cadaver if he was determined to do so. The cases we have available today were discovered either because the bodysnatcher was observed in the act of exhumation or was caught trying to transport the cadaver on the next express coach to Edinburgh. Leaving a body above ground to decompose over a number of weeks may have acted as some form of deterrent, but if such a grave was opened in error, the teeth or a less well decomposed body part might have been removed and subsequently sold to the right buyer.

However proficient and wily the public believed bodysnatchers to be, newspapers often mocked them. Cases of mistaken identity, of student pranks and of sheer stupidity provide a glimpse of the true character of some of the forgotten bodysnatchers and the scrapes that some of them got into when trying to procure a cadaver.

Chapter 5

Punishment

Dealing with the perpetrators

'. . . as it now stands . . . it[s] only a misdemeanour, that is to say a crime punishable by a fine and imprisonment , as a common assault is, or as a libel is, to steal, to sell or to purchase a dead human body.'
      – William Cobbett, *Political Register*, Volume 75 (1831).

No one was immune from prosecution for stealing a dead body. Yet, very different sentences were awarded according to the defendant's status in society. Anatomy lecturer Granville Sharp Pattison was severely reprimanded in 1813 for stealing the body of a Mrs McAllaster, whereas bodysnatcher and reputed thief Harry Perring was sentenced to three months' hard labour in 1822, after stealing a body from St Mary's Churchyard, Newington.

As a dead body did not count as real property and therefore did not belong to anyone *per se*, stealing a corpse was classed as a misdemeanour; a crime was only committed if property belonging to another person was taken. Any bodysnatcher worth his salt always routinely threw the burial shroud into the bottom of the coffin before the soil was replaced. If they were caught taking any item from the grave, including the coffin and/or its fittings, this could be classed as a felony and the bodysnatcher might be punished accordingly.

In 1795 Sir John Fredrick failed in his attempt to get a Bill through Parliament to upgrade the crime of bodysnatching to a felony and so it remained a misdemeanour, right up until it all but faded out with the passing of the Anatomy Act in 1832. Potential punishments ranged from whippings, severe reprimands and fines to straightforward imprisonment and even, on occasion, transportation. The type of punishments delivered by the authorities fluctuated.

A very early case of bodysnatching in which a punishment is recorded occurred in Edinburgh in 1739. Colin Rhind, a mason, was found guilty of opening the grave of Mary Stewart who had been buried in the West Kirkyard. An easy target for the resurrectionist, West Kirkyard (later known as St Cuthbert's) would be so plagued with bodysnatchers that the authorities erected an 8ft wall around its perimeter and also established a watch there in 1803. Rhind was sentenced 'to be carried to the Cross, there and at Cowhead Well, West Port, and at the end of Portburgh, to receive on his naked shoulders three stripes.'

Another early case of bodysnatching also earned the punishment of whipping. In 1777, John Holmes and Peter Williams, together with a female bodysnatcher named Esther Donaldson, took the body of Jane Sainsbury from St George's Churchyard in Bloomsbury. Holmes was the gravedigger and Williams his assistant, whilst Donaldson was 'charged as an accomplice'. All three stood trial for the snatching of Jane Sainsbury. Holmes and Williams were not only sentenced to six months' imprisonment but also whipped 'twice on their bare backs, from the end of Kingsgate Street, Holborn, to Diot Street, St Giles, being half a mile'. Much to the authorities' annoyance, there was insufficient evidence to convict Esther Donaldson.

Further lashings of the whip were delivered on the streets of London two years later in relation to another bodysnatching case, which occurred at St George's, Hanover Square. John Powel was publicly whipped in January 1779, as well as receiving six months' imprisonment. The crowds loved watching a whipping almost as much as a hanging. Bystanders in Midlothian were not to be disappointed in 1742, when bodysnatcher John Samuel was tried for stealing the body of Gaston Johnston from Pentland Kirkyard. Samuel had been caught as he tried to enter the city of Edinburgh with Gaston's body tucked under his arm. His was to be a harsher sentence than some, for not only was he publicly whipped through the streets of Edinburgh, but he was also banished from Scotland for seven years.

Trials involving students and doctors who had perhaps ventured into a dark churchyard but were a little slow in making their escape, show an altogether more lenient outcome. When bodysnatching was in its infancy, certain members of the medical profession believed that they were above the law. Few took measures to try to hide the fact that they were carting dead bodies around the streets at night, in order to furnish their dissecting tables the next day. In 1788 a London surgeon named Lynn was fined a paltry ten pounds, after he was tried for stealing a female body from St Saviour's churchyard. The authorities had finally started showing their dissatisfaction with those surgeons who involved themselves in such a base occupation.

There was no consensus as to the punishment a surgeon or student might receive if found guilty of bodysnatching, as the case of Henry Haley Holmes shows. Holmes's choice of cadaver was rather disturbing. Described as a surgeon by the newspapers, Holmes was charged with having broken into a vault in Hendon churchyard on 13 September 1828, along with accomplices James Wood, a bricklayer and Charles Charsley, 'a lad' and cut the heads off three bodies. This strange and macabre story is quite unique, yet the reasons Holmes gave for his actions still applied directly to the advancement and development of medical understanding.

The Spectator stated that Holmes 'had been only actuated by a passionate devotion to science' when he removed the heads. It later transpired that this was for the sole purpose of phrenology; that is to study the shape and size of a skull in order to better understand the subject's personality traits.

Holmes's father had previously spoken to the vicar of Hendon, Rev. Theodore Williams, claiming that he wanted to enter the vault so that he might 'select the scattered bones of his relatives, and put them in a decent form.' An unusual request, but one that was duly granted nonetheless. When the clerk noticed that the coffins within the vault had been tampered with and the heads from three bodies removed, Mr Williams travelled directly to London to 'bring the offenders to justice'. The Holmes family apparently possessed a 'particular complaint of the brain' and they had hoped that Holmes Junior would be able to discover the cause of the affliction through the study of phrenology.

One witness questioned during the trial, John Conolly a hairdresser from Hendon stated that as he passed the churchyard when he was heading to work he saw:

> 'the defendant remove a shroud from a body, and raise the body up and support it with something which he held in his hand. [He then saw] Holmes hold a knife in his right hand and cut the head off the dead body. [He] then removed the skull to the further end of the coffin, and put it into a blue bag. I could see there was hair and flesh on the first head that he [Holmes] took.'

At the trial, Mr Alley, acting in Holmes's defence, gave him a glowing character reference and 'wished to take the liberty of stating . . . the defendant's ardent pursuit of science'; an observation that was probably taken into consideration during sentencing. All three men involved in the 'snatching' were found guilty of their misdemeanour, with Wood and Charsley fined five pounds each. It was recommended however, that Holmes was shown mercy on the grounds that 'merely his love of scientific investigation' had motivated the act. Holmes was fined twenty pounds.

But what about the strange underlying factors in this case? During the trial it transpired that there had been no interments in the vault for a number of years. Perhaps the most shocking evidence that came to light was that Henry Haley Holmes, avid supporter of medical advancement, had stolen his own deceased mother's head.

Two apprentices from Huddersfield got off slightly better than Holmes when they were tried in 1827. John Beaumont was apprenticed to the apothecary at the Huddersfield Dispensary, whilst his friend, John Barker was apprenticed to a surgeon and apothecary. Their quarry was the body of 12-year-old Thomas Ellam, who had died during an accident at Lockwood Reservoir. As later described in the *Leeds Mercury*, by 'dying in full health and vigour, a larger price would be obtained for the body . . . as disease had not [weakened] it, the muscles being in proper order'.

Thomas was buried at St Peter's Church on 30 November, but his corpse would turn up in a box on the back of the Leeds coach two weeks later. On the night the two apprentices raided St Peter's it was raining and not a particularly promising evening for a bodysnatching expedition. Beaumont was wearing light-coloured trousers and would have had some difficulty in getting them clean again after their muddy work. The pair removed Thomas's body and took it back to the dispensary, situated at the back of the Pack Horse Inn (now the Packhorse Shopping Centre).

At their trial, Thomas Balderstone, a machine-maker from Huddersfield, explained how he was in the yard at the back of the inn, having a drink, when he heard the two men approaching. He recalled that 'one was deficient in his walk, and the other had on drab trousers'. When morning came, Thomas was already packed into a box 'about a yard and a quarter long' and weighing 'about four or five stone'. He was placed on the roof of the Leeds coach, with Beaumont as his companion. The journey must have been fraught. Beaumont clutched the box throughout the twenty-mile trip and when Edward Aspinall the coach driver asked him about the contents and whether or not the box really did contain a dead body, Beaumont explained that it was an 'electrifying machine'.

Electrotherapy machines, which administered an electric shock to the patient, were already being used by the early 1800s to treat conditions such as epilepsy and Beaumont had one on his knee, or so he said. The machine was to be taken to Dr Thackray in Leeds, he explained, to be mended. On the return journey, Beaumont confessed to the coachman that he had indeed guessed correctly and that there was a dead body in the box, 'but don't tell anyone'.

Amongst the original trial papers and notes a few things stand out. When Thomas Balderstone gave evidence at the Wakefield Quarter Sessions in January, he mentioned that 'one [of the bodysnatchers] was deficient in his walk'. This was a key identifying trait and a list was prepared as part of the evidence showing all the men who walked with a limp in the neighbourhood. There were seven in total, although one was later crossed off the list.

The other interesting piece of evidence lodged amongst the solicitors' papers is a brief noting that Dr Thackray purchased Thomas's body but he 'subsequently sent it back to Huddersfield on the solicitation of the deceased's friends [having removed] some of his intestines (see copy minutes of the examinations taken by the magistrates)'. Unfortunately, these copy minutes are no longer available, but one has to wonder why Thomas's friends thought it permissible for Dr Thackray to remove the boy's intestines before sending his corpse back.

A note written in the margin of one of the solicitor's briefs states that an electrifying machine was sent to Leeds to be mended at this time, and that 'the prosecutor has been seeking up evidence to prove that it did not go by Beaumont'. The notes made by the solicitor in the margin also read 'but with what success it is not known'. This has subsequently been crossed through.

At the summing up of the trial, the jury was told:

> 'the present indictment against two young men, members of an honourable and useful profession, and one which they should have every assistance to qualify themselves for the situation they were to fill. It was a stigma which might stick to them through life, and therefore they would not convict them unless upon the most satisfactory evidence.'

Both apprentices were found not guilty of stealing the body of Thomas Ellam.

As the decades wore on and professional bodysnatchers began to dominate the scene, they too would be tried and fined, often with much harsher penalties than their medical associates. It was not uncommon for a surgeon to look after the families of the resurrectionists who had provided him with corpses, if they were sentenced to imprisonment, or to try to have their sentences reduced. When Joseph Grainger was caught stealing the corpse of John Fenton in October 1831, from Smethwick Churchyard near Birmingham with fellow bodysnatcher Benjamin Sandbrook, he had already served six months for bodysnatching three years earlier.

At Grainger's first trial, he and bodysnatcher John Watts were tried for stealing the body of Richard Clarke from the burial ground at Tipton, Birmingham. Things didn't go well, despite a petition being sent to the Home Office signed by five medical men, including surgeon William Sands Cox of Birmingham Medical School, the pair were sentenced to six months' imprisonment and fined ten pounds each.

Grainger's second jail sentence of six months' imprisonment with hard labour and a ten-pound fine was delivered once again after William Sands Cox had signed a petition requesting leniency. This time two petitions were received by the Secretary of State regarding Grainger and Sandbrook, consisting of an individual petition by Sands Cox regarding Grainger alone and a petition signed by seven lecturers of Birmingham School of Medicine and Surgery regarding both bodysnatchers.

Sands Cox's petition, dated 4 July 1832, requests clemency and shows that Sands Cox was supporting Grainger's family throughout his imprisonment:

'the term of his [Grainger] sentence is now expired, and I most respect-fully trust that your Lordship under existing circumstances may be pleased to recommend to his Majesty to remit the fine. As lecturer on Anatomy at the Institution, I have been compelled my Lord to defray the law expenses and to support his wife and children for the last eight month . . . when your Lordship considers the evidence on which the individual was convicted and the heavy expenses which have fallen upon me, a young man commencing his profession I am led to anticipate that your Lordship will take the circumstances into your consideration.'

A letter from Sir Oswald Mosely, Chairman of the Quarter Sessions for the County of Stafford, shows that he also disagreed with the severity of the pun-ishment: 'I am sorry to observe that the Court of Quarter Sessions exceeded their powers by annexing the punishment of hard labour to the sentences passed upon Grainger and Sandbrook.' Grainger's petition has been annotated 'nil', suggesting that his fine of ten pounds was replaced by the additional punishment of hard labour.

Sandbrook was given an altogether more lenient sentence of one month's imprisonment with hard labour, even though he had played an equal part in the snatching. Joseph Grainger's harsh sentence was passed by the same magistrate who had sentenced him in 1829, so perhaps he was not convinced that Grainger had learnt his lesson.

Sometimes it is easy to see why a criminal received the sentence they did. In the case of night-watchman John Walker the sentence of transportation was certainly deserved. In 1748, Walker was tried at the Old Bailey for 'stealing a Coffin, value 3s. and a shroud, value 2s. the property of Joseph Wright'. Having secured the body of Francis Hill from the gallows after he was hanged for bur-glary – denying the surgeons one of their legal cadavers – Wright took Hill back to his lodgings, where he was to be prepared for a decent burial.

When Hill was secured in his coffin, Walker, together with associates, later broke into the house and stole not only the dead body but also the coffin and shroud, quickly bundling everything into a waiting coach. A neighbour alerted Joseph Wright that some men had stolen Hill's body away and that he was 'sold to a surgeon and that his head was cut off and that a woman who sold dog and cat meat told her so'.

Wright went to the surgeon's house to investigate and sure enough, there was Francis Hill laid out on top of the coffin 'with his head off'. Joseph Wright confronted Walker about his part in the 'snatching' and he divulged that he had 'sold him for a guinea, three shillings for a coach and half a crown to drink'.

As previously mentioned, the stealing of grave clothes was considered to be far more serious than the act of bodysnatching. In 1824, Essex bodysnatcher Samuel Clarke was tried for stealing the bodies of 24-year-old Joanna Chinnery, 30-year-old Susannah Knight and 33-year-old Abraham Leader. He was also tried for stealing a shift, gown, night-cap and a pair of white stockings – the grave clothes belonging to Joanna Chinnery.

After removing the body of Joanna Chinnery from her grave in St John's churchyard in Little Leighs, five days after her burial, Clarke had hidden her body under a hedge with a view to transporting it at a later date. Yet, Clarke's downfall began when his horse and cart were found tied to a tree in a field alongside the turnpike at Little Leighs. The cart was taken to the nearby Castle Public House and left with the landlord, Mr Crisp. Two hours passed before Clarke came to claim the horse and cart. When he arrived, Clarke claimed that he had been drinking throughout the previous day and had been sleeping off his excesses, only to wake up and find his horse and cart missing.

In the meantime, local blacksmith Robert Broomfield, decided to investigate the area where the cart had been found. A shovel – some accounts also include a crowbar – and a folded sack containing a brace of pistols were discovered and, under a hedge, slightly buried in soil, Broomfield unearthed the naked body of Joanna Chinnery. Broomfield immediately sought Mr Simmons, the owner of the land on which the body had been found and the current churchwarden. Simmons had been present at Joanna's burial only a few days prior and immediately recognised her. The hunt was now on for a bodysnatcher and Clarke was apprehended while leaving Little Leighs, having just been reunited with his horse and cart.

At the inquest Clarke was adamant that he had had nothing to do with the whole affair. Yet, upon further investigation a box stowed under his cart was discovered to have the 'most offensive odour'. It was easily large enough to store a couple of human bodies. Clarke was charged with stealing the grave clothes of Joanna Chinnery and sentenced to seven years' transportation, still protesting his innocence.

Interestingly, a bodysnatcher named Samuel Clarke turns up seven years later in Roydon, thirty-six miles away from Little Leighs. Charged with stealing a dead body at the winter special assizes in 1830, Samuel Copper (alias Clarke) was sentenced to six months' hard labour. When called upon for his defence, Clarke stated: 'I am a resurrection-man, and am obliged to get my living by it. What would the surgeons do, my Lord, without me? I have been a great sufferer through it, and I hope the Jury will be favourable to me.' If this is in fact the same resurrectionist, then his previous punishment had had little effect.

In 1829, James Bell, described as 'of that class called 'Resurrection Men', and three associates were convicted of breaking into the house of Daniel Redday in Deptford and stealing 'therein a shirt, a worsted comforter, and the body of a black man whose name was unknown'. The deceased was lodging at Redday's house when he became unwell and died suddenly on 19 November. His body was duly laid out in one of the back rooms with 'the shirt on, and the comforter round his head'.

During the night, however, Redday heard a noise in the room where the corpse was and fearful of coming face to face with a burglar, he went outside to see if he could spot anything untoward. When he reached the side of the house, Redday saw a set of ladders leaning up against the house, directly under the room occupied by the corpse. Four men were on the ladder, one of whom was James Bell. Realising they had been spotted, the men tried to escape. In their haste they fell to the ground, with the corpse landing on Bell, pinning him to the spot. When sentence was passed by Mr Baron Garrow he stated 'it was at the best interests of society, [to] sentence him [Bell] to transportation for life'.

* * *

Some bodysnatchers felt that they were providing an irreplaceable service to the anatomists by procuring corpses with no questions asked. The risk of a prison sentence was only a minor deterrent. In February 1826, bodysnatcher Michael Armstrong was questioned about his part in the snatching of 15-year-old Martha Oddy from Armley churchyard, Leeds, having asked the gravedigger how deep he was planning on digging her grave and who exactly was going to fill it.

Armstrong's six-month term of imprisonment in York Gaol did little to dissuade him from his bodysnatching career. One year later, when he was arrested again in Cheltenham, this time on a charge of vagrancy, on being asked by the magistrate how he provided for himself, Armstrong wrote his reply on a piece of paper. Handing the folded note to the bench, he was anxious that it remained secret. Nonetheless, the court reporter from the *Cheltenham Chronicle* managed to discover its contents. The press divulged the full contents of the note, and the text was subsequently published in local newspapers throughout the country.

The *Morning Post* ran a small but poignant article about Armstrong's case with a full transcript of his note: 'Honoured Sir – I supply the different annatommicle [sic] Schools in London with Subjects Constant but no one knows me hear except 2 or 3 of the surgeons.' Armstrong was sentenced to one month's hard labour in Northleach House of Correction.

Scotland also sentenced its bodysnatchers to transportation and had its fair share of repeat offenders. Thomas Stevenson, alias Hodge, was banished for seven years after being found guilty of stealing dead bodies from Larbert church-yard, Stirlingshire, in 1823. Bodysnatching was an unpleasant occupation at the best of times but to hide your quarry in a dung heap in order to collect it later must have seemed unappealing to even the most seasoned bodysnatcher. Hodge had been seen with another man removing packages out of a dung heap and placing them in a cart. Realising they had been discovered, the two bodysnatch-ers fled for Linlithgow but were soon surrounded by an angry mob. One of the bodysnatchers made a run for it, leaving Stevenson a sitting duck in possession of three noxious cadavers.

In a broadsheet covering the trial it was reported that Stevenson had 'previ-ously been convicted under the name of Hodge'. Two years prior, Hodge had been convicted of violating the churchyard in Lanark and stealing two dead bodies with the help of bodysnatcher Andrew Miller. In this complicated case Miller and Hodge were linked to an incident in Currie, nearly twenty-seven miles from Lanark, in which two supposed 'peat-dealers' had been seen twice on the same road with a loaded cart. Two labourers, who had seen the pair became suspicious, so they followed them to Ravelrig toll house where they were seen 'wishing luck' in the form of a toast, to the contents of their cart, which had a 'putrid smell proceeding from it'.

The labourers, suspecting illicit dealings, fetched the local excise officer who found the bodies of an old man and woman concealed within the cart. Both cadavers were recognised as having been recently buried in Lanark churchyard. There was nothing to prove that Miller and Hodge had exhumed the bodies themselves, aside from the fact that they were in possession of them. The result of the trial, as the Lord Justice Clerk pointed out, was 'in consequence of it [the jury] having not proved that they [Miller & Hodge] were the actual per-petrators of the offence.' Being found guilty nonetheless, both Miller and Hodge were sentenced to six months' imprisonment.

However, the judge delivered a stark warning to the bodysnatchers that 'the Court would not in future be inclined to look on their offences with so lenient eye.' Hodge apparently did not heed this advice and two years later he suffered the consequences.

If a bodysnatcher was apprehended and the locals found out, their reactions towards these men and women invariably showed their disgust for the profession.

A number of cases resulted in the accused bodysnatcher being attacked while merely moving between gaol cell and court room, as well as accounts of the populace sacking the homes of those involved before proper evidence had been collected. The 1742 riots in Edinburgh demonstrate just how incensed the public could become if they heard rumours of the final resting places of their families, friends and neighbours being targeted.

In 1829, after the arrests of William Yeardley and Mary Steward (alias Cox) in Barnsley, South Yorkshire, the local populace was so outraged that the police officers had difficulty in protecting the pair while moving them to the cells after appearing before the magistrates. The hostility remained unabated, even though the magistrate would later rule that the body had been snatched from Sheffield, rather than a local churchyard.

The mob that followed bodysnatcher William Hodges from the watch-house in Poplar to the Lambeth Street Magistrates in 1822 was frenzied to say the least. An 'immense and infuriated' mob followed Hodges to the court 'pelt[ing] both him [and the watchmen brought into restrain them] with mud and every sort of missile that they could get their hands on'. The officers unfortunately took as many hits as Hodges himself. When Hodges did eventually get into court, Magistrate Mathew Wyatt asked him if he was the 'resurrected' or the 'resurrection man', as he looked as white as a ghost.

Once parishioners heard that a bodysnatcher had ventured into their parish there was often no stopping them from taking matters into their own hands. In April 1823, the mob was still so incensed with Stirling bodysnatchers James McNab and Daniel Mitchell, after the case against them was dismissed, that the pair had to seek refuge in the gaol that they had just been released from. Such commotion was caused by one bodysnatcher being detained in Glasgow during 1823, that it was necessary for the constable to tie both the bodysnatcher and the cadaver together in order to safely take him into custody.

If a mob managed to gain access to a dissecting room, the scene before them would have stayed with them perhaps for the rest of their lives. The mob entering the lecture rooms at Duke Street, Glasgow in 1823, witnessed the following grisly tableau:

'On the floor stood a large tub, in which was found a number of heads, arms and legs. On the table lay the whole body of a woman with long hair. The body of a man lay aside it with the head cut off and entrails out, and otherwise dissected. At the end of the room was a complete skeleton. Other mangled bodies were found and limbs and mutilated fragments of bodies.'

Enraged, the mob 'seiz[ed] the bodies and everything found in the room, [and] tossed them into the streets', before they set about demolishing the building.

* * *

An accusation of bodysnatching was a serious matter, and on at least one occasion a former bodysnatching suspect claimed compensation for the resulting stain on his character. In 1828, five men were tried at the Lancaster Assizes near Warrington, with 'conspiring to disinter and take away the dead body of Jane Fairclough', who had recently been interred in the Hill Cliff Burial Ground. Three of the men; Edward Hall, a surgeon and apothecary, Richard Box and Thomas Ashton were acquitted, whilst William Blundell and John Davies, a 'student at Dr Moss's dispensary' were fined five pounds and twenty pounds respectively.

Jane's body had been found in Dr Moss's dissecting room, 'perfectly naked in a hamper', after his 'respectable student' John Davies had asked if he could bring a young subject home with him. The case is unusual because of the actions for false imprisonment Richard Box brought against three men: Peter Nicholson, an attorney; Paul Caldwell, the keeper of the Bridewell; and James Joynson, a constable in Warrington.

Box stated that the three men came to his premises on the night of 3 October and accused him of assisting in stealing a dead body. Box was then taken away to the Bridewell, where he spent the night. Upon his release, he had to walk through the streets with the fear that the populace could turn on him at any given moment, if they discovered what he had been accused of. The *Liverpool Mercury* wrote of the case:

'It was no light matter to be subjected to popular irritation . . . working on the ignorance of persons who were not aware of how important it was, for the preservation of health, that medical men should have opportunities of dissecting the bodies so of the dead.'

As these sentiments were not shared by the general populace at this time, no wonder Box felt apprehensive walking home. There was little or no evidence to suggest that Box was involved in the snatching and, as a warrant was never produced, Box firmly believed that he was being accused out of malice by Nicholson the attorney. Box had been implicated because Dr Moss's servant had said that Box was one of the men who had brought the hamper containing Jane's body to the dissecting room.

Before any evidence could be given by Box's solicitor, the magistrate called a halt to the proceedings, as he felt it was clear that malice had not been intended, however 'it was clear there was no legal apology for their conduct.' It didn't take the jury long to reach a verdict and, to 'a considerable sensation in court', Box was awarded damages of fifty pounds.

There were greater risks, however, than mere loss of reputation for professionals and falsely accused bodysnatchers alike. A number of bodysnatchers were wounded, or even killed, while trying to scrape together a living. When bodysnatchers attempted to steal the corpse of James Howlett in 1828 from his final resting place in Bacton churchyard, Norwich, they had a surprise waiting for them. When suspicions were aroused after a man had been noticed asking about Howlett's burial, the village decided to set up a watch on his grave consisting of six men.

Sure enough, in the middle of the night two bodysnatchers drove up to the churchyard wall in a gig and made their way slowly over to Howlett's grave. While they were occupied in lifting the 'sod from poor Howlett's head' shots were fired by the watch. The watch peppered one bodysnatcher's legs with shot and this proved sufficient to scare the pair away. The injured bodysnatcher stumbled back over the churchyard wall and made his escape into the night, whilst his companion drove the gig away from the scene 'with all possible speed'. Newspaper stories rarely offer much more detail than this and many bodysnatching stories remain frustratingly unfinished.

In Bedminster churchyard in 1822, a melee between bodysnatchers and constables resulted in noses being broken and rapiers being drawn. At the beginning of November, six men were caught trying to exhume a recently buried corpse. Such was the struggle at the grave-side that one of the bodysnatchers was hit in the nose with the butt end of a pistol. Their trial took place at the Somerset Quarter Sessions in Wells and the five 'young gentlemen of this city' were indicted not only for 'disturbing and digging a grave' but also for 'assaulting one of the patrol in execution of his office' and for 'assaulting the chief constable . . . with the intent to rescue another of the conspirators'.

The 'gentlemen', who turned out to be medical students, were concerned about their forthcoming punishment in case it 'might prevent them being admitted as surgeons', but they need not have worried. After admitting to all of the charges except the conspiracy to raise dead bodies, (this section of the charge being removed) and, after considering the implications of the sentence on the future careers of the five men, the men were all found guilty of 'assaulting one of the Patrole in the execution of his office . . . effecting the rescue of one of the conspirators . . . assaulting the Chief Constable [and] 4thly for a riot and assault'.

The judge then addressed the jury:

> 'Hippocrates, Galen, and the most distinguished surgeons were indebted
> for their great attainments to the science of anatomy, which could only
> be acquired by dissection are very forcibly observed upon what the
> feelings of the husband, parent or friend would be, who saw the object
> of his affections writhing under the most acute agonies, who could not
> be relieved unless medical men had the opportunity of investigation
> and experience, which were only to be acquired by dissection.'

The jury waited until the next assizes to pass full sentence, hoping to have
been able to discuss the case with other judges. In the meantime, the five 'gentlemen' were bound over with sureties of one hundred pounds each.

Of course, like any criminals, some bodysnatchers would try to talk their way
out of arrest. The four men apprehended in Islington in 1817 were no exception. Having been discovered with a dead body in their possession, the men
were escorted by the watch to the watch-house, where they were asked to explain
themselves. With great ingenuity they set about explaining that the body they
had with them was actually being taken to be buried and they had certainly not
dug it up. They also casually mentioned that the corpse had died of typhus.
The hint of infectious disease was enough to clear everyone from within the
watch-house in a matter of minutes. The constable on charge immediately
informed the prisoners that they were indeed free to go and that no charge
would be brought against them 'desiring them to quit the watch-house without
delay'.

The bodysnatching cases reported in the press involved resurrection men and
students who were caught in the act or seen violating graves. Hundreds, if not
thousands, of empty graves throughout Britain will forever remain the secret
targets of bodysnatchers. Only they knew which churchyards they targeted and
why, which graves were emptied and how easy it was to remove the corpses.
Only they could tell us which surgeons they supplied and how much money
they made.

The prosecutions mentioned here are the more unusual cases. The majority
of snatchings that were detected ended up being punished with either a fine
and/or a prison sentence, and these cases generally do not make for entertaining
reading. What was common throughout, however, was the tendency for the
surgeon to safeguard their supplier. Without resurrection men, surgeons and
their lucrative anatomy schools would not have been able to function at the
capacity they did and British students would have trained abroad, where they
could be guaranteed a cadaver on which to practice.

The legal supply of cadavers was woefully inadequate and the violation of Britain's churchyards was becoming too much for the public to bear. Something had to alter dramatically to improve the situation. It was clear that medical students needed to study the human body, but where were they going to get the quantity of cadavers they required?

Chapter 6

The Trials of the Solicitors' Clerk
The case of John Craig Hodgson

'In the coffin were an iron bludgeon and a glove. Holes had been bored in the coffin lid to admit a saw, and a piece had been sawn away from the head to the breast. . . The instrument [bludgeon] *was loaded with lead at one end, and at the other was a piece of blue listing to attach it to the hand.'*
– *Leeds Intelligencer,* Thursday, 17 November 1831.

Bodysnatchers did not always take to the trade out of necessity, as events that played out in West Yorkshire in 1831 proved. The men involved in this case did not need to sell cadavers; some of them were employed in white collar jobs within the community and had promising careers ahead of them. Yet, a solicitor's clerk and a schoolteacher would become linked with the macabre underworld of bodysnatching, their future careers ruined as a result.

John Craig Hodgson had secured a position in Leeds as clerk to Matthew Gaunt, an 'Attorney of his Majesties Court of King's Bench and solicitor in the High Court of Chancery' and was nearing the end of his five-year term when he took an altogether different path. Hodgson had grown up in the city; his father was a cabinet-maker and the keeper of the Regent Inn in Kirkgate. Hodgson had progressed well with Mr Gaunt, until he received a criminal record for stealing the body of Thomas Rothery from Wortley churchyard in 1831.

Fifty-nine-year-old Thomas Rothery was buried on 29 May 1831, after he was killed during an accident at work. He worked in the dye house of Messrs Scarth and Sons and had been scalded to death after falling into a vat of hot dye.

But why was a Yorkshire solicitor's clerk stealing bodies? Thought to have previously studied medicine in Edinburgh, Hodgson had failed to qualify and instead retrained as a legal clerk. He cannot have been immune to the goings-on of the bodysnatchers during his time in Edinburgh and must have understood the amount of money that could be raised by procuring corpses for the dissection table. Perhaps the prospect of financial gain attracted Hodgson to begin dealing in cadavers?

Whatever reason he had for adopting this course, Hodgson's plan went awry. His very first bodysnatching raid was discovered, when the stolen corpse was found wedged underneath the stairs in an office located on the corner of Albion

Street in Leeds. A report in the *York Herald* stated that two men with a horse and cart had been seen in the vicinity of the Episcopal Chapel in Wortley on the night of the snatching. The witness, another attorney's clerk from Leeds, had overheard a conversation between the men standing by the cart relating to the surgeon who was soon to be in receipt of the body.

Unfortunately for Hodgson, the surgeon was not in a position to accept the goods at that time and a decision had to be made about where the recently exhumed corpse of Thomas Rothery was to be stored. The office chosen belonged to Hodgson's employer. Following the snatching and the information given to the chapel warden, notices were put up throughout Leeds offering a five-pound reward for information leading to the culprits. Investigations soon led to Hodgson and the police paid him a visit the day after he had exhumed the corpse.

Hodgson answered the door to the police himself when they called round. Naturally concerned that his employer would find out the truth about his illicit dealings, Hodgson confessed to the snatching almost straight away. Thomas Rothery's body was found tightly packed into a box, already wrapped in canvas ready for shipment. A piece of leather acting as an address label was attached to the front of the box, which read: 'Books – Please keep dry – The Rev. William Dixon. Mail Coach Office. Carlisle, June 2nd 1831: per coach.'

Hodgson was tried at the Leeds Borough Sessions and labelled in the papers as 'a young amateur anatomist'. He gave his own defence, which was ridiculed by the press, the *Hull Packet* describing his speech as 'amazingly long; and like most things extended over a large surface – weak.' Hodgson received a six-week gaol sentence in York Castle, after he admitted to working with a man in the medical profession, although he refused to divulge his associate's name.

It didn't take long for Hodgson to return to bodysnatching after his release. His brief confinement in York Castle did little to diminish his desire to provide cadavers to the medical fraternity. Within six months, Hodgson was once again being tried for bodysnatching. This time he had apparently enjoyed more success, as the press stated that he was supplying cadavers to medical men throughout the country.

Towards the close of 1831, Hodgson was arrested as the ringleader of a six-strong bodysnatching gang. The two cadavers Hodgson's gang snatched in November of that year appear side by side in the burial register for East Ardsley Church. Both were male, one a small boy of four named Joseph Langley Fielding and the other Robert Hudson, a young man of seventeen, who had hanged himself in the cabin of the coal house where he worked. When Robert's body was found, the *Bury and Norwich Post* mistakenly reported his death as a 'supposed case of murder for anatomical purposes'. The press seem to have been preying on the public's fear of 'burking', following the recent scandal involving

Burke and Hare in Edinburgh who had carried out numerous murders to supply the anatomists' tables with cadavers.

The body of Robert Hudson, despite being packed securely in a box, caught the attention of the police when it was about to be placed on the Courier coach bound for Carlisle. After opening the box and confirming that there was indeed a body stashed inside, neatly packed with sawdust, Robert Hudson's corpse was taken to the Court-House Yard in Leeds so that a formal identification could be made. The press reported '1000's of people' looking at the body, but it was not identified until 'after a very long investigation'.

Robert Hudson had been buried in East Ardsley churchyard on Tuesday, 1 November, with little Joseph Langley Fielding following him to the grave the next day. The snatching of the two cadavers occurred on the night of Friday, 4 November. The sexton, Jonathan Bedford, went to Hudson's grave on 5 November and noticed that it had been disturbed. On opening the grave he found 'some linen and an iron bludgeon'. The bludgeon was about 12in long, with a 'handle of iron or steel . . . there was a blunt knob or globe at one end, filled with lead, and there was a blue ribbon to put round the wrist. It was a most formidable weapon'.

He also noticed that 'the lid [of the coffin] had been cut by a saw across the shoulder' and that the 'coffin plate which belonged to Robert Hudson's coffin was found in the coffin of the adjoining grave'. The following day the sexton also noticed that Fielding's grave had been disturbed and found that his coffin was empty.

The Leeds gang standing trial at the Northern Circuit of the assizes that November consisted of: John Craig Hodgson, articled clerk to an attorney at Leeds; John Crabtree Pickering, a schoolmaster from Bond Street, Leeds; William Germain, a packer from York Road, Leeds; William Henry Bradley, a joiner from Leeds; James Norman, a butcher from Wade Lane, Leeds; Thomas Pearson, a cloth weaver of New Road End, Leeds; John Wood, a shoemaker from Buslingthorpe, near Leeds; and Henry Teale, a gentleman's servant from Moor Town, Leeds. All of the accused had respectable, if not lucrative jobs yet they were all somehow lured into the macabre world of bodysnatching.

When Henry Teale, the gentleman's servant, was called to give evidence, Hodgson appeared troubled, making objections to him being in the stand. Although part of the gang, Teale was to turn King's evidence in an attempt to reduce his own sentence and his statement proved damning for Hodgson. At the time of the snatchings, Teale stated that he had been unemployed for nearly a year and was currently working as a labourer. Hodgson had approached Teale in the Blakewell Ox public house, asking him whether or not he was in work. When he learnt that

Teale was in 'reduced circumstances', Hodgson told him that he could help him 'find something by which he could get a comfortable living.'

A few days later, Hodgson would tell him about the resurrection business. During the trial, Teale openly admitted that he had agreed to work with Hodgson and went on to inform the court that he had been given a piece of paper from Hodgson detailing all the churches that he was to visit, so that he could note which graves had recently been prepared. There were a number of 'rounds' detailed on the list, confirming that the gang was targeting several different churchyards in the local area. The gang would meet by appointment, at different public houses which [were] named when they settled where they were to go to fetch subjects'.

Further questioning showed that Teale and gang member William Henry Bradley both visited East Ardsley churchyard after the name of the church appeared on Hodgson's list. When they arrived, they noted two graves that had recently been prepared 'at the back of the church, about fifteen yards from the footpath'. These were the graves of Hudson and Fielding. After reporting their findings to Hodgson later that night, it was decided that they would go and 'fetch' the cadavers and two gigs were duly hired.

When they were within a mile of the churchyard, the gigs were driven into a nearby field and the gang continued the rest of the way on foot, taking their tools with them. Entering the churchyard alone, Hodgson made sure that the coast was clear, before signalling to the rest of the gang to enter. Teale started digging at 'the small grave', that is Fielding's grave, whilst William Henry Bradley concentrated on 'the large one', the grave of Robert Hudson. When Fielding's coffin was reached, Bradley broke open the lid while Hodgson continued to dig in the larger grave.

Bradley then 'placed a rope around his [Fielding's] neck and drew the body out of the coffin, the others assisting on drawing it out'. Teale set about stripping Fielding of his burial clothes, throwing them back into the grave and stuffing Fielding's small, clammy body into a sack. Whilst Hodgson and Bradley focused their attention on trying to reach Hudson's coffin, Teale replaced the soil he had excavated from Fielding's grave making the area appear untouched.

The party arrived back in Leeds between 2am and 3am and shortly afterwards the two graves were found to have been disturbed. Both bodies were taken in separate sacks to a garden house belonging to James Norman's parents, where the process of getting them ready for shipping could start. Hudson's body was packed first and was secured in a box, which was subsequently covered over with canvas. The label was written out and the box was taken at 5.30am to the Times Coach Office. However, Hodgson's carefully laid plans would now start to fall apart, for the coach had already left, meaning that Hudson's corpse had to be returned to the garden house, located on Woodhouse Lane.

The gang then turned their attention to the body of Joseph Fielding. His small body was packed, ready to be shipped on the courier coach the following evening, addressed to 'M Quay, Surgeon's Square, Edinburgh'. The body of Joseph Langley Fielding was never seen again.

James Norman's father was understandably unhappy about the fact that there was a dead body lying in his garden house and he asked if it could be removed. A few weeks previously, schoolteacher John Crabtree Pickering had hired a house in Tobacco Mill Lane in Sheepscar, to the north-east of the city, in order to assist the gang in transporting cadavers on the various coaches leaving for Edinburgh. However, unbeknown to any of the gang members, the owner of the house was in the process of negotiating a sale on the property and the new owners wanted a final look inside before signing the papers.

In an unfortunate turn of events, the box containing the body of Robert Hudson had been refused transport on the coach for a second time, after the gang had tried to transport his body to Edinburgh a few days later. The driver refusing to accept delivery of the box containing Robert's body because of the pungent smell and, as a result, it was now being stored in the house on Tobacco Mill Lane. If Hodgson had not panicked and urged Pickering to remove Hudson from the house in such a hurry, then perhaps they would have got away with their snatching.

However, Pickering was seen hurriedly leaving the house with the box. William Penniston, the owner of the Tobacco Mill Lane house raised his suspicions to a constable, after seeing Pickering together with gang member James Norman, taking the box to the Courier coach at the Rose and Crown Inn. When examined, the body of Robert Hudson was found inside the box labelled for collection by 'Hon. B. Thompson, Carlisle'. The label had been hastily written out on the back of a ticket for the Leeds Philosophical Lectures.

When Pickering was arrested, to his horror the house was searched and a selection of bodysnatching paraphernalia was found. A spade, gimlet, bloody sack and 'various other implements' were noted, along with a book and a ticket to the Philosophical Lectures both of which were in Hodgson's name. A paper found on the premises during the search was also inscribed with 'a triangle, under which were Hebrew characters, for the words, THE BONES – then followed '*John Hodgson. Missionary*'– at the bottom was a crucifix.

In the middle of the investigation into Hodgson and his gang, the 'Hon. B. Thompson' received another package. It was intercepted at Carlisle after arriving on the coach from York. Noticing 'a very suspicious-like package', the police officer on duty opened the box and found stuffed inside the naked body of a 'fine boy, about fourteen years of age'. The body was rumoured to have come from Leeds.

Other cadavers were also being discovered in the coach offices of the city whilst Hodgson's case was being investigated. The Bull and Mouth public house in Leeds detained a box arriving from Manchester on 11 November. It contained the bodies of an elderly lady and a two-year-old child. It was addressed to 'The Rev. Mr. Geneste, Hull, per Selby Packet; to be left until called for. – Glass and keep this side up. Nov.11th'. The identity of the two cadavers remains unknown and their bodies were re-interred by order of the coroner. For passengers travelling by coach through the North of England, the possibility of sharing their journey with a corpse seemed to be increasingly likely.

Hodgson's trial continued, despite the bodies now turning up all over Leeds. After successfully representing himself at his trial for violating the grave of Thomas Rothery, Hodgson once again took to the stand. He questioned Dr Thomas Chorley's diagnosis that the body of Robert Hudson showed signs of strangulation, suggesting that instead the body showed signs of apoplexy, arguing that it would be difficult to arrive at this theory with the body in such an advanced state of decomposition.

Hodgson also questioned Constable William Halton, regarding the slip of paper containing the drawing of a triangle and Hebrew characters. In an attempt to gather further information, Halton had shown the note to people in a number of different public houses in the area. According to one of the men he interviewed, the note was in fact 'Hodgson's oath – that the triangle meant secrecy, the Hebrew characters stood for dust, and the crucifix signified that they were sworn on the Holy Evangelists to disclose no secrets; that if any of them should be apprehended getting a body, they were not to inform, for if they did they would be in peril of their lives'. When this information was disclosed in court, Hodgson remained silent.

The number of items found by the police in the house in Tobacco Mill Lane left no doubt that all five men – Wood and Pearson having already been discharged – had been involved in the exhumation of both Robert Hudson and Joseph Fielding. The evidence listed at the trial included:

'. . . two hay spades, one larger than the other; a brace and bit, a gimlet; an iron hammer; a red jacket; a fustian jacket; a hat lining that had been used as a cap; a pair of overalls; a small saw, which might be converted into a knife . . . two sacks; a blue bag; a carpet bag, a right hand leather glove, two address cards taken from the box, the one directed to the 'Hon. Benj. Thompson, Mail Office, Carlisle' the other to the "Hon. Benj. Thompson, Mail Office, Edinburgh, to be left until called for".'

The presence of the two jackets proved to be important. When Henry Teale was re-examined during the trial he admitted that he had 'forgotten to mention' that Hodgson had in fact put on a fustian jacket when he'd left the gig as well as a pair of gloves, to go into the churchyard and that he himself had put on a red jacket, together with some overalls'. All of these items had been recovered by the police.

More damning evidence was to appear when Thomas Flockton, the constable and clerk at East Ardsley Church, produced a second glove that he had seen thrown out of Robert Hudson's grave on the night in question. The glove was examined and was 'the fellow glove' of that found by the police. Joseph Langley Fielding's mother, Elizabeth Fielding, gave evidence that she had not been aware of any disturbance when she had visited her son's grave two days after the funeral. However, when she was shown a cap by a neighbour who said that she had found it near Joseph's grave, Elizabeth knew it was the same cap that her son had been buried with.

'Is it not possible for me to get my child back again?' Mrs Fielding asked the magistrate. 'There is no hope of it being discovered,' was the solemn reply. With this first part of the examination completed, the bodysnatchers were bound in sureties until the next assizes.

At the Northern Circuit of the assize court in April 1832, the trial of John Craig Hodgson, John Crabtree Pickering, William Henry Bradley, William Germain and James Norman, all aged twenty-five or under, began at 1pm. It would be another six hours before the case for the prosecution closed, Hodgson's address to the jury alone lasting over two hours.

By the end of the trial, Pickering, the teacher, had been ordered to stand down due to the lack of evidence linking him with the exhumations, whilst the remaining four men faced prison sentences, as well as fines. Despite bringing both his sister-in-law and brother to the stand to report that he had been at his father's house in Potternewton on the night of the snatching, Hodgson was still found guilty. Perhaps it was due to his tirade, in which he 'set about charging the press with having lent itself for the purpose of maligning and injuring him', or his claim that Teale had been paid off 'for the express purpose' that he might lose his liberty. Either way, Hodgson lost his case.

When sentence was passed, Hodgson's lack of legal knowledge, despite his training as a solicitors' clerk, was deemed 'astonishing':

> '. . . one is really astonished that you should make the speech and defence you have, and knowing all that you should, put into the box your sister in law and brother to commit perjury on your behalf . . . it does not lessen your guilt in the least, on the contrary, it aggravates it. Under these circumstances I must pass upon you a more severe sentence than I shall do upon the others.'

John Craig Hodgson was 'imprisoned for one year and to find four sureties for good behaviour for two years, in the sum of £50 each, and . . . imprisoned until such sureties be found'. When sentence was passed, it was discovered that Hodgson was already under recognizances to keep the peace in relation to stealing the body of Thomas Rothery the previous year.

The remaining three men, Bradley, Germain and Norman were considered to have been 'led into this affair' with no real intention of becoming bodysnatchers. The punishment given to these men was a warning to other amateur bodysnatchers. All three were imprisoned for three months in Wakefield House of Correction, after which each of them had to find sureties for the sum of ten pounds each.

Hodgson does not appear to have been linked with any further bodysnatching cases, but that does not mean that he disappeared from the pages of history altogether. In the 1851 census returns for the district of St Andrew's, Manchester, a John Craig Hodgson appears, living in a 'Model Lodging House' on Brown Street. Aspiring to a better class of lodgers, the model lodging house was a cut above the mixed sex lodging houses which were often filled with disease. These superior lodging houses aimed to improve the standards of cleanliness of the lodgers' quarters and to oversee the morals of inmates. Hodgson, then aged forty, is recorded as married and born in Leeds. Noting his occupation as 'Attorney 'Out of Practice', Hodgson ensured that the secret of his criminal past was safe for a little while longer.

By 1861 Hodgson appears to have made his way to London and is recorded in the census returns for St Giles in a lodging house at No. 2-4 Potts Place. John C. Hodgson, now referring to himself as a solicitor from Leeds, is noted as a 50-year-old widower. Although some reports indicate that Hodgson had died by 1868, there appears in the 1871 census returns for Clerkenwell Workhouse at Holborn Wood, a solicitor from Leeds named John Hodgson, aged sixty-three, who is described as a lunatic.

* * *

The trial of the Leeds bodysnatching gang caused a sensation in its day. Nothing like this had been witnessed in the North of England on such a large scale before and the police kept a reminder of the macabre events. Photographs of John Craig Hodgson's home on Elmwood Street, Leeds, dubbed 'Resurrection Cottage', is preserved by Leeds Libraries and you can view it on their Leodis website.

Chapter 7

'For the Purpose of Gain and Profit'
The case of Henry Gillies

'On Wednesday week an extraordinary sensation was excited in . . . the whole of the town of Manchester, by the alleged discovery of a gang of monsters, who were supposed to rival Burke and Hare in the number and atrocity of their crime'

– *Leicester Journal*, Friday, 22 April 1831.

Henry Gillies was a well-known figure amongst the medical students in Glasgow, supplying those students who were too delicate or too busy to perform snatchings themselves. Employed as a gravedigger in Calton Burial Ground, his employment came to an abrupt end when he was found to be re-selling coffin furniture to local undertakers. But Henry Gillies dealings with the macabre underworld did not end there and would eventually take him far beyond the city walls of Glasgow into the criminal underworld of Manchester.

In 1820, Henry Gillies was indicted on two counts at the Northumberland Lent Assizes; the first for 'breaking the soil of the Tynemouth Churchyard and taking up and carrying away there from the body of some person unknown' and also for 'stealing dead bodies for the purpose of gain and profit'. The snatching had taken place just before New Year's Eve 1819 in the small parish of Tynemouth. Although Gillies may have stolen the bodies for 'gain and profit', the *Assize Kalendar* [sic] of February 1820 put forward the view that he had also stolen the cadavers 'for the purpose of dissection'.

Renting a room in a lodging house at the Wooden Bridge, North Shields was perhaps the easiest step Henry Gillies had to take in order to set up as a body-snatcher. Moving boxes to and fro without your landlady noticing was a little harder, but people moved items all the time and the three men lodging with Margaret Charlton in November 1819 did not appear to want for money. As long as the rent was paid, why should Margaret get involved?

However, she still kept an eye out, observing that Gillies and his two associates sent 'away three boxes about a yard long and half a yard wide'. Gillies kept regular hours, his landlady discovered, except when he went to Newcastle, 'once or twice at nights.' Red boxes were not that common in North Shields, yet at a similar lodging house not too far from Wooden Bridge, landlady Isabella Sprott also noticed red boxes appearing on her premises. Gillies had come to visit his associate Graham and, after what must have been a successful meeting, turned up the following day with three large red boxes and one small.

The comings and goings of the two men started to arouse Isabella's suspicions and on the morning of 24 December, Gillies called for Graham at 5am. When the pair returned to the house, they went immediately upstairs to Graham's room and it was not long before a red box made its appearance downstairs, all corded up ready for delivery.

Elsewhere in the parish little escaped the eye of the curate of Tynemouth Church, the Rev. C. Barnes. In a small parish with a close knit community, the appearance of a stranger would have been remarked on. Henry Gillies had already been spotted 'hovering in the churchyard during funerals, not as a mourner, but as a looker on' by the Rev. Barnes on more than one occasion.

Other people had also spotted Gillies' suspicious behaviour. Cabman James Hussick was standing at the quayside in Shields on 29 December, when he saw Gillies approach in a boat with two other men. The boat was heavily laden with a large box. Hussick operated a gig between Shields and Newcastle and approached Gillies to ask if he could be of any assistance. Gillies replied that he wished to travel to Newcastle taking the box with him. The usual fare for such a journey – a distance of thirteen miles – was two shillings. Gillies offered Hussick three shillings and increased his offer by a further sixpence if he would set off for Newcastle immediately, without waiting for any more passengers. Hussick agreed and arrangements were made to drive to the Bird in Bush Inn in Newcastle, rather than putting the party off at the quayside.

Arriving at the inn around midday, Gillies was hoping to transfer the box straight onto a carrier for Edinburgh, but George Scott an agent working on the wagons, had other ideas. Scott was suspicious about the contents of the box and wanted to open it before it was loaded onto the coach. The *Caledonian Mercury* described the box as red, 'there being no other of the same description in the warehouse'. Scott's instincts had been correct, for when he opened the box it did indeed contain a dead body. An old woman was tucked neatly into one of the large boxes en-route to Edinburgh.

Eight boxes had already passed through the Bird in Bush Inn according to Scott, and when he had calmed down after his most recent discovery, he sent for the churchwardens of Tynemouth parish who, it was hoped would be able to identify the body. The corpse was that of 'a slender old woman, [who] appeared to have been recently interred' and she was quickly identified as local resident 79-year-old Mrs Buck, who had been buried only the day before in Tynemouth churchyard.

On 17 January 1820, a meeting was held in Tynemouth Church between the 'vicar, churchwardens and gentlemen of the four and twenty and principal inhabitants of this parish', following further information received from Edinburgh: 'A letter from the police officer in Edinburgh having been read to the meeting announcing that Henry Gillies the person suspected of abstracting bodies from the churchyard was in custody there.'

They had got their man, but Gillies protested against the charge, saying, 'It [was] an unlikely story that he should come to this part of the country' and asking, '[why] should I use my real name and say I came from Scotland if I had come on bad design'. Gillies's protests did little to help him and the magistrate hinted that Gillies ought to be found guilty of 'breaking the soil of the Tynemouth churchyard and taking up and carrying away from there the body of some person unknown'. With regard to the second count, 'stealing bodies for the purpose of gain and profit', the jury was urged to consider whether or not Gillies had in fact taken up the body and if he had, could they be certain it was going to be used for such purposes.

The jury found Gillies not guilty on the first count, but guilty on the second. A twelve-month imprisonment in Morpeth Gaol was his punishment, together with a twenty-pound fine.

Eight years later, Gillies was to be brought to justice once again when the night of 17 March 1828, during the early hours of St Patrick's Day, the parish watch of Anderston heard footsteps approaching from the far end of town. James McDougall, together with three other watchmen, Donald McMillan, John Horn and Finlay McLean, were in the middle of their night's watch when all four men heard the sound of footsteps proceeding along North Street, Anderston, just outside of Glasgow. They were coming from the direction of Main Street, which ran across the top of North Street, alongside the New Burial Ground.

There was no urgency in the footsteps, but the watchmen judged from the number of steps heard, that they were about to face a group of men rather than a lone individual. It was likely that anyone out on the streets at 3.30am would be up to no good, especially a group of men. Meanwhile, the men also became aware of the nearby watchmen and decided to toss two sacks containing 'some heavy substance' over a hedge into a nearby garden. They may have got away with this, had garden not been diagonally opposite the watch-house on the corner of North Street and Sauchiehall Road.

As they drew nearer, watchman James McDougall noticed that there were four men in total, walking two abreast and that one of the men walking at the front was taller than the others. This small detail was to be crucial in identifying

Henry Gillies. As the four men walked past the watch, Daniel McMillan shone a light in the direction of the taller man at the front. All of the watchmen had seen this man throw two sacks over the hedge and they wanted to know who the culprit was. As soon as the light was at the height of the taller man's face, he turned around. His face now lit up by the lantern, McMillian was able to make out the features of Henry Gillies, 'from his flat nose to his broad head.'

The four bodysnatchers responded quickly to the watchmen's actions. As McLean and Horn went to investigate the contents of the sacks, McDougall and McMillan gave chase. McDougall seized Gillies almost immediately, whilst trying to dodge a punch from one of the other bodysnatchers during the tussle. The other bodysnatchers ran off in all directions, with the 'boxer' amongst them heading in the direction of Glasgow.

'What have I been detained for?' asked Gillies, adopting a surprised manner.

'You might easily know,' replied McMillan. He recollected in court that 'the smell he [Gillies] had [about him] . . . was as intolerable from the prisoner as the corpses which I [McMillan] had immediately before seen.' Henry Gillies must have been so used to digging up cadavers that he had become immune to the stench.

The unfortunate Gillies had been taken to Anderston Police Office, along with the two sacks, which had been rescued from the shrubbery and loaded onto a cart. As soon as the group had arrived at the station, the sacks were open and suspicions confirmed. Two bodies were found squashed inside the canvas, 'the corpse of a grown woman and the other the corpse of a child'.

It didn't take long for the evidence against Gillies to start pouring in. Whilst questions were being asked at the station, all four watchmen had returned to the scene of the crime to search for clues in the immediate area. They were not disappointed for, after a short time, a spade was found just outside the garden gate to another house a short walk over the crossroads past the garden into which the sacks had been thrown. Produced as 'Exhibit A' during the trial, it was noted that the soil sticking to the spade was the same as the soil clinging to 'Exhibit B', Gillies's shoes, which had been removed when he arrived at the police station.

Witnesses at the trial included William Dick, a weaver who was also the Bailie for the middle division of the New Burial Ground. He recalled that following the interment of a female child of Margaret McNeill's (neé Weir) on 17 February, he had visited the grave not long after but there was no sign that the earth had been disturbed. However, on hearing that two bodies had been found, he immediately went to the burial ground and discovered that: 'there had been lifted the body of Robina McNeill by taking it out through a hole on the right side and near the head of the coffin. Also the body of an elderly woman which had been taken up through the fracture at the head of the coffin.'

Unfortunately, William Dick was unable to identify the second body because as:

> 'the coffin was one given by the Sessions it must have been that of some poor person, and no record [was] kept of such. That this last mentioned body was in such a state of putrefaction and decay that no person could recognise or identify it.'

Samuel McCluer, however, thought that the elderly woman 'came from somewhere about Springbank or Broadside and had been interred five months ago'. The body of Robina McNeill however was 'quite entire and was at once recognised by the mother'. Marks left on her body after 'two leeches had been applied to her breast' shortly before her death also helped with her identification.

When Robina's mother Margaret was called to the stand, she was able to verify this theory. Her mother-in-law Elizabeth McNeill, obviously nervous of the resurrection men, had gone to the burial ground 'immediately after the funeral and put a private mark over the grave'.

Following the snatching of the two female corpses, Dick and McCluer both stated that a third cadaver was taken out of 'the second grave'. It was the corpse of an infant girl who had been buried in the evening of Friday, 7 March by her mother Jean Galbraith. At the trial, Jean Galbraith confirmed that she had buried a daughter that day and that 'the child died on 7 March at about five o'clock . . . that the said child never was baptised nor got a name.'

When she heard of the snatching, she immediately went to the grave and noticed that it had been disturbed and that 'the coffin was lying at the side of the grave . . . that a little white wrapper of cotton cloth, a small cap . . . and a white muslin handkerchief were all the dead clothes and they were lying at the side of the grave.' Gillies had most certainly known to remove the burial clothes from the cadaver to avoid prosecution for theft.

Gillies had, however, committed another cardinal sin for a bodysnatcher by making a nuisance of himself. Dick had 'seen him going in and about the said burying ground, and had on different occasions put him out of the ground from being suspicious of him and from having heard that Gillies was a body-lifter'. Dick was shown 'Exhibit A', the spade, which he called 'peculiar to a body-lifter because it is more easily concealed by being shorter in the handle. [I am not] aware that any regular grave digger use any such spade'.

A stick was also produced which had been found at Gillies's home. Dick noticed that the soil sticking to it was the same as that on the spade and the shoes. He had seen 'holes made in the graves', no doubt with 'a view of ascertaining the depth at which the coffins lay in the graves and [that] the said holes were of the same size as if they had been made with the stick now shown . . . [He] had particularly observed a great number [of holes] within the last two or three weeks'.

Finally, Gillies's former colleague at Calton Burial Ground, James Dunn, gave evidence as to his unsavoury character. In the six months that Gillies had worked at Calton Burial Ground in 1823, rumours had started to spread that there was to be an attempt made to lift dead bodies from the graveyard. Dunn, suspecting Gillies's involvement, confronted him at his home where he stated he 'found Gillies' shoes besmeared with soil corresponding with that from which the bodies had been attempted to be lifted'. Dunn also noted that a spade matching the description of 'Exhibit A' had also been found in Calton Burial Ground that night.

Agnes Sinclair, who had been married to Gillies for 'about five years', tried to provide him with an alibi for the night in question. She told the court that the pair had been sitting at the kitchen table at their house in Carmichael Land, Glasgow, when a 'young man who she thought to be a student and who was dressed in a long blue coat, slender made' arrived at their home. He was 'accompanied by [another] two men' and he went up to her husband and 'spoke something in a low tone of voice to him.'

Agnes was asked to confirm whether she had seen the shoes shown to the other witnesses, but she declined to look at them. When shown the stick, Agnes said that it belonged 'to her husband's uncle John Henderson a travelling packman who stays in McLellans Land, New Wynd, Glasgow'.

The stick, as well as a length of rope also produced in court had both been found at Gillies's house when it was searched by William Graham a Sheriff Officer in Glasgow. While searching, Graham also came across a hollow compartment in the floor, in which was 'a small collection of water and blood and the stench of the apartment was exceedingly strong and inoffensive'. When Janet Mitchell, a lodger in Gillies's house and his supposed mistress, was called as a witness all hope of a reprieve was gone.

Recounting the scene when Gillies was visited by a man in a 'long blue coat', whom he called 'Peter', Mitchell went on to say the he 'has often been out during the night . . . it is a common report in the neighbourhood that he is employed in lifting corpses.' She then mentioned that the man in the blue coat had been seen repeatedly at Gillies's house, along with other men, 'one of them who is said to be a surgeon called Mr Christie'.

According to Janet, the morning following the snatching, 'Peter' went to Gillies's home to inform his wife that 'he had been out with her husband the preceding night lifting some dead bodies and that her husband and two of the bodies had been taken and carried to the Anderston Police Office. That Christie was very grieved for Gillies.'

Henry Gillies naturally contradicted Janet. His job at Calton Burial Ground was poorly paid, he said, and this was the real reason he had left the job. His work until about three weeks ago had consisted of making 'feathers for the caps of the private soldiers about the town'. He was adamant that he had not been in the New Burial Ground in Anderston and claimed that he had given the false name of Harry Henderson when arrested, because 'he was averse to giving his real surname on account of the crime laid to his charge.' The spade was the type used to dig children's grave according to Gillies, but he had never used one like that himself. He declined to answer questions about why he had been abroad at that hour.

Henry Gillies, according to police officer Donald McLean, was reputed to be:

'. . . a corpse lifter, [who] has been taken up ten or twelve times within the last year on charges of lifting, and his house has been repeatedly searched on suspicion of having dead bodies in it. [They] have not known of any lawful employment that he has had during that period or for months before – he has never been convicted of any charge of corpse lifting – though he has been convicted of assaults and twice in Bridewell on such convictions.'

The outcome of this trial is unknown, but it is likely that Gillies received at least a few months' imprisonment. Whatever his punishment, there was no reforming such a nefarious character as Henry Gillies, who was to be linked with another macabre event a few years later, this time in Manchester.

'On Wednesday last, an extraordinary sensation was excited in Oxford Road . . . by the alleged discovery of a gang of monsters, who were supposed to rival Burke and Hare.' So began an article in *The Standard* published in April 1831. According to the paper, word of the dramatic events witnessed by the inhabitants of Aughton Street, or 'Little Ireland' as it was locally known, had spread through the town 'like wild fire, embellished with a thousand absurd exaggerations'.

A ten-year-old girl had been walking home late one evening when she happened to glance in through the kitchen window of No. 7 Oxford Road. There she observed an old woman, concentrating on the work in front of her. After catching sight of a blade in the woman's hand, working back and forth stripping the flesh from a dead greyhound which was lying on the table, the girl scampered off, telling everyone she met on her way what was taking place in the house down the road.

A crowd soon formed and demanded to be let into the woman's house so that they could see exactly what was occurring. But the occupant, Amelia Anderton, 'who could speak nothing but Gaelic,' refused to let the mob in. Although she managed to stave them off for a short period, the mob eventually gained access to her kitchen and they were shocked by what they discovered. Hidden in the pantry was a jug full of water, inside of which was the skeleton of a small child, 'the whole of the flesh having been removed from the bones.'

That was not all, *The Standard* claimed: 'Small bones, part of the finger of a child, a singular looking instrument . . . and on a quantity of shavings in a corner of the room, was found a female infant in a weak state of health.' Alarmed by this, the mob launched themselves at Amelia and her daughter-in-law. The daughter-in-law managed to escape, but more bones and a skeleton were found during the melee, further fuelling the fire.

Fearful that murder would be committed, the landlord of the property called in the police and Amelia was taken to the police station, along with the collection of bones. Later that evening, a man walked into the police station in an intoxicated state, kicking reporters as they attempted to get a story for the evening edition. The man was Amelia's son and he knew all about the 'murders'. He gave his name as Gillies.

According to the *Bristol Mirror*, Amelia was 'a miserable looking creature whose son was a resurrectionist'. At this point, *The Standard's* description of her became even more derogatory: '[she] presented a miserable specimen of age and decrepitude . . . and in her appearance alone, would in a former age have been accounted sufficient to support a charge of demonology or witchcraft.'

As soon as Gillies walked into the police station he stated he was 'a resurrectionist and an articulator in skeletons' and 'had a countenance peculiarly repulsive and forbidding.' The *Bristol Mirror* noted that Gillies was 'employed by several surgeons in that town [Manchester] in making anatomical preparations.' When sentenced to find bail and two sureties of twenty pounds each, Gillies stated that 'his employer would at once give bail for his appearance,' further strengthening the claims made by the press.

Soon after the examination a gentleman of 'high professional character' confirmed Gillies's statement and assured the public that he had not been involved in anything untoward. The body of the infant found in the jug of water was a stillborn infant and had been 'used in the dissecting room'. It was Gillies's job as an articulator to prepare the skeleton for anatomical purposes and for this he received one pound per week. The work was usually done in the lecture rooms rather than at Gillies's home, for the reaction of the populace if the work was discovered, would be problematic. But such was the character of the Scottish bodysnatcher that he didn't heed the advice of his superiors and had removed the body to his lodgings.

The description of the 'singular looking instrument' found at Gillies's home by the mob, sent the minds of the newspaper-reading public into overdrive. The newspapers labelled it as a 'blood sucker', used to suck out the blood from unsuspecting children. They were nearly right. It was identified in the *Leicester Journal* as a 'syringe of peculiar construction' used in blood preparations. 'A mix of wax and other compounds are injected into the veins of a subject, so as to represent blood. These are [then] used in the illustration of lectures on the blood vessels.'

If the mob had found out what the instrument was really used for, Amelia would probably not have got out of her house unscathed. One can never be quite certain as to the truth behind the statements printed in historic newspapers and consideration must be made to the amount of potential exaggeration. This case was perhaps exaggerated through the works of the 'catch-penny publishers', who introduced the story that Gillies and his mother Amelia were 'a regular gang of Burkites, who made a regular trade in killing children for the purpose of converting their flesh into *meat pies!*' Other scandal sheets reported that 'a plentiful supply of these delicacies had been supplied at Knott Mill Fair.'

Chapter 8
A Catalogue of Errors
When snatching a corpse did not go to plan

'We expressed some grave doubts as to the truth of this story.'
– Evening Paper, Wednesday, 8 December 1824.

Bodysnatching stories, like many tales from the eighteenth and nineteenth centuries, have on occasion become distorted and the true facts are difficult to trace. Many of the cases reported in the newspapers have been re-worked, not only by contemporary writers but also by researchers.

Stories become intertwined and it is common to hear of tales 'unique' to a particular parish, only to discover them in a slightly different format as folklore for a parish one hundred miles away. Tales once retold by parish elders often recount grim occasions on which bodysnatchers raided the local area, but rarely give specific details and have often been pieced together from other fireside tales passed down through history.

The stories that have been recorded for posterity usually give the reader the grimmest of details, in an attempt to escalate the horrors of the bodysnatchers' crimes. The press often helped to fuel the fear of bodysnatching, playing up relatively minor facts, and this could have severe consequences. In the early hours of Friday, 13 June 1823, a man was seen walking along Piccadilly (or Pall Mall, depending the account you read) in London. Slung over his shoulder appeared to be a dead body wrapped in a sheet. He was soon followed by a crowd and, to the utter terror of the bystanders, a human arm suddenly flopped out of the sheet.

The assembled crowd soon became convinced that he was a bodysnatcher and started to shout abuse and a 'volley of invectives' at the man. He was finally apprehended and taken to St James's watch-house for questioning. However all was not what it seemed. When the sheet was untied it did contain a body, but not a human one. The figure inside the sheet was made of cork and dressed in female clothes. The supposed bodysnatcher was a tailor and the cork dummy was used as a model to make lace dresses.

Shortly before Christmas 1828, a box measuring 16in inches deep, 16in wide and 3ft 1in long was made ready for collection. Tied with cord and fastened tightly with screws, it was addressed to a 'Mr Mackenzie, Lecturer of Annatomie [sic], University, Edinburgh'. The box was placed to one side ready for collection and the landlord of the Wheat Sheaf in Castlegate, York, employed a porter to collect the box and take it to the coach office so that it could be sent to Edinburgh on the High Flyer coach later that day.

By 1828, most observant coach drivers knew what a 'suspicious looking box' looked like and the box addressed to Mr Mackenzie showed all the signs of containing something untoward. The coach driver refused to accept the box and told the porter to take it back 'to the place from whence it came'. He was, however, advised to take the box to the police instead. By the time he had reached the Guildhall news had spread of the suspicious package and a large crowd had gathered, with someone having grabbed a list of recent interments in St Sampson's churchyard, in order to try to identify the potential victim squashed into the box. The crowd had soon decided that the unfortunate cadaver must be Mrs Hebden, who 'had been committed to dust' the preceding Friday.

'One might have taken a guinea to a china orange that the body of the deceased would be locked and screwed in this *mysterious box*' stated the *York Herald* and, as the crowd gathered round whilst the box was opened, 'attitudes prepared to shrink with the start of fear.' Suddenly, the atmosphere changed. Smiles broke out across the faces of the fearful bystanders, as the smell emanating from the box was finally identified as coming from four cured hams, which had been carefully packed ready to be sent to the 'Lecturer of Annatomie [sic]' in time for his Christmas dinner.

Bodies for dissection were hard to come by and the opportunity to get hold of any subject that could be dissected was usually acted upon. In 1826 the *Edinburgh Courant* reported on a 'most disgraceful attempt' of a porter trying to convey a dead body into the medical school on College Street, Glasgow. The man was seen walking carefully in through the gates of the college, but he was stopped by several members of the public before he could get inside. The crowd accompanied the man to the police office so that they could witness him being questioned.

Dr Black, a surgeon at the College Street School was called for so that he could examine the corpse fully. Whilst they waited for Dr Black to arrive, the sack was opened and, according to the *Courant*, 'it was found to contain – we shudder to write it – the corpse of that interesting and innocent animal called by Mr. Wombwell, the *Lama*.' The lama had died in Mr Wombwell's menagerie and it was being taken to the College for dissection. According to the newspaper report 'few remained to see the final commitment of the porter or the disposal of the dead body.'

In addition to cases of mistaken identity, graveyards also played host to the odd prank, especially during the haunting month of October and the night of All Hallows' Eve. Even bodysnatchers were not safe, as this story, published in the *Edinburgh Observer* in January 1823, reveals:

> 'In our Monday's publication we mentioned a humourous [sic] mistake committed a few nights before in this neighbourhood, and we now wish to amuse our readers with an *éclair cissement* [sic] of a somewhat similar event that befel [sic] two disturbers of the dead. . .'

Having settled down to an hour of digging in an unnamed churchyard, one of the resurrectionists became concerned that there was no one to hold the horse to stop it from wandering off. Suddenly, an answer came from an 'elfin groom' who came up to the cart after 'skipping across a grave' and declared, "I'll haud the horse lads!" Naturally the bodysnatchers scarpered from the scene 'like maniacs,' leaving their horse and cart to the would-be spirit. The spirit was in fact a local youngster who had settled down for the evening under a table tombstone. The horse and cart were sold for a handsome profit, which was apparently sufficient to send the youngster to school.

The country bodysnatcher's trusty horse and cart played a part in a number of scares. A country doctor, returning home after spending the day on house calls, happened to pass by the parish churchyard and observe two bodysnatchers at the grave of one of his recently deceased patients. Hiding in the shadows, the doctor watched as the corpse was taken out of the grave, covered in a dark cloak and arranged on the front seat of the gig, so that the grey, sickly-looking cadaver would appear to be one of the party.

The journey started off well, with no apparent problems, until one of the bodysnatchers commented, "The body seems to be warm still." "So it is," the other replied. Nothing more was said until the doctor, having swapped places with the cadaver replied, "Warm! And if you had been where I have been for the past twenty-four hours you would be warm too!" Leaping from the cart, the bodysnatchers made a run for it, once again leaving their transport to be claimed by the prankster!

Not all bodysnatching attempts aimed to source a cadaver for the dissecting table. In 1822, Denbigh in North Wales was the target of a very unusual break-in. The men involved in this case were driven by greed. Thomas Jones Esq. had lain in his vault for just over one year before he was disturbed one Friday night in February by a gang of 'seven or eight men'. Perhaps if the gang had been a little more careful they may have been able to carry out their plan without being detected, but evidence of their activity was noticed the following Sunday morning.

A year of decomposition had taken its toll on Mr Jones's flesh and gruesome evidence of his attempted exhumation had been left on the grass outside of the vault. The 'stains and the smell' instantly alerted the clergyman and church-wardens that something was wrong. The body would have been useless to the anatomists however, so why did the gang target the vault of a man who had been dead for over a year? It is said that one of the 'resurrection men', supposing that he had been mentioned in Jones's will, had dreamt that there was a copy of it nestled under the cadaver's head and that his intention was simply to retrieve it.

Perhaps the strangest case of cadavers being snatched and used for purposes other than dissection appeared in the May 1796 edition of *Universal Magazine*, of a 'man who shewed beasts in Tyburn Road' in London. He did not steal bodies himself but obtained them from 'the fellows who stole them from Cripple-gate churchyard'. The dead bodies were just as important to him as they were to the anatomists, for the menagerie-keeper was using them to feed his 'wild beasts'. The mob seemed quite vexed at the thought of this and it was with great difficulty that he was committed to the New Prison.

* * *

When it comes to students carrying out their own raids a number of different stories have been recounted. From more genteel backgrounds than the profes-sional bodysnatcher, students who had a mind to procure their own corpses for dissection often needed to strengthen their resolve with a drink or two, in order to get the work done. One particularly unfortunate event occurred after five students had fortified themselves en-route to a graveyard in Coull, Aberdeenshire, in 1827.

One of the students came from the area and had been in the village the previ-ous day whilst a local farmer had been buried. When meeting his fellow students later that night, he confidently reported that, "No watcher's out, but the min-ister's windows are showing light; he'll be having his Sunday night toddy by now and should be snoring in bed soon."

After a short wait, the coast was clear and four students made their way over to the farmer's grave, whilst one looked after the horse and cart. The digging commenced, two keeping watch as the others worked hard at shifting the freshly turned soil. Suddenly, a dog barked excitedly, causing the students to leap behind the nearest tombstone. Just as quickly as it had started, the dog calmed down and the students carried on digging for their subject. They had managed to successfully remove the farmer from his grave and get his corpse over the churchyard wall when they were spotted.

Dumping the corpse in a nearby turnip field the five students ran in various directions, resigned to losing the body they had so recently exhumed. But the watchers gave chase and soon they had the bodysnatchers in their sights. Shots were fired and a squeal was heard. "You've murdered a student Tam," cried one of the watchers. "Run lads run or we'll hang for this night's work." Unbeknownst to the watchers, they had actually shot the minister's pig.

Stealing a cadaver and then going for a celebratory drink at the local inn also made the basis of a popular tale, which is told in relation to many different parishes. Two students would steal into a quiet graveyard, quickly exhume a cadaver. Then, having secured it in a sack and returned the grave to its original condition, they would nip into the local public house.

One such story reportedly involved Robert Liston, later an eminent Edinburgh surgeon, and a student friend of his. Together they are said to have raided the churchyard of Leven in Fife where they stole the body of a man named Henderson. During the raid, one of them became ill and needed to stop at the nearby inn. Whilst resting upstairs, they overheard a conversation in the bar regarding a theft in the village and, realising that they needed to make a hasty retreat, escaped through an open window, leaving the corpse concealed in another room. When the landlady came to retire for the evening, she climbed into bed only to be greeted by the cold clammy body of her recently buried husband.

One of the most unfortunate stories of student grave-robbing concerns three students who raided the Blackfriars Kirkyard in Glasgow. Having successfully stolen a corpse from a grave, while they were heading out of the kirkyard one of the students was fatally shot, after he caught the wires of a trip gun and set it off. His friends had no desire to leave their fellow student's body lying in the kirkyard, so they tied their legs together, as if in a three-legged race and hobbled back home, pretending to be in high spirits. They put their friend's body into his room and started a rumour that he had committed suicide. There is no record of what happened next, but this frequently re-told story may have been enough to scare off would-be bodysnatching students.

One popular bodysnatching tale involves a cadaver coming back to life after being dug up by bodysnatchers. Both Penicuik and Gilmerton in Scotland lay claim to the same tale, but exactly where it originated is not entirely clear. The story follows three students on their journey out of Edinburgh, as they embark their first bodysnatching raid. The students were naturally nervous, as this was to be their first bodysnatching attempt and problems were bound to arise. One of the students kept guard in case they were discovered and held the horse so that it would not wander away, while the other two proceeded to dig up the body of a recently buried female parishioner.

The first problem they encountered was when they realised that they had forgotten to bring anything with them in which to carry the corpse. There was no alternative but to take a deep breath and hoist the body up onto the shoulders of one of the students. Unfortunately, the student started to lose his grip on the cadaver as he was walking out of the churchyard, allowing her clammy form to slide slowly down his back until her feet were scraping along the floor. When the corpse's knees started knocking against the back of the student's legs, he cried "She's Alive, She's Alive, My God She's Alive!" The petrified student dropped the cadaver and raced out of the village with his friends.

In the morning, so the story goes, the husband of the deceased lady found her lying in the road not too far from the churchyard and naturally thought that she had escaped from her coffin after being buried alive. It was a long time before the widower was convinced that his wife had in fact been the target for the resurrection men.

Regrettable incidents like this did not just befall unprepared students. The quiet burial ground at Hume, Berwickshire was the target for two bodysnatchers who were hoping to steal a potentially valuable subject. The deceased was a man in the prime of his life, who had left behind a wife and young family. The evening after the funeral, the widow of the deceased made her way down to her husband's graveside to spend a few quite moments in contemplation. When she arrived in the churchyard, however, she spotted two men digging soil from her husband's grave. Without thinking, she snatched a spade that was lying nearby and with all her might brought it down on the head of the nearest bodysnatcher. She must have brought it down with some force for the other bodysnatcher immediately took to his heels and ran off into the night.

Overcome by her actions, the young widow then fainted only to wake in the early hours of the morning, bemused by the evening's events. The grave of her husband appeared untouched and the two mysterious bodysnatchers were never seen again. The two men in question were rumoured to have been the local gravedigger and a servant who, on fear of being recognised, had fled the area.

Many years passed with no more thought given to the episode until the lady herself passed away and wanted to be buried with her husband. When the grave was opened once more, lying just beneath the surface was a 'mouldering uncoffined skeleton' of one of the bodysnatchers. Still intact beneath the skeleton was her husband's coffin buried all those years ago.

'Fresh' cadavers were also occasionally the subject of jokes played on unsuspecting surgeons by resurrection men. After bodysnatchers had dropped off a sack containing a corpse in the usual place for Dr Brookes, owner of the private anatomy school in Blenheim Street, London, they made their way to leave.

Dr Brookes was standing at the bottom of the stairs, however, and he asked them why they had not brought the sack all the way down. Two bodysnatchers caught hold of the sack and after they had only moved it a short distance, the top of the sack came open and a 'living subject threw his naked arms and legs out, and begged for his life'.

Dr Brookes immediately armed himself with a brace of pistols and demanded to know what was going on. The 'corpse' explained that he had come from Teddington in Middlesex just that day and had got so drunk that he did not know where he was. He had no recollection of the events that had brought him there and was at a loss to say what had taken place. In reality, the naked man worked for the resurrectionists and he had been asked to climb into the sack as a bit of fun!

* * *

Perhaps the saddest error made by a group of bodysnatchers occurred in 1823, when a bodysnatcher accidentally lifted a member of his own family. The incident was reported in a number of newspapers including the *Staffordshire Advertiser*, under the heading 'A Caution to Resurrection Men', and is said to have occurred in a 'St Martin's churchyard' in an unconfirmed location. Body-snatcher 'Simon Spade' was exhuming a corpse one night in January when he realised that he had made a dreadful mistake. Looking into the face of the cadaver and brushing back the hair, he realised that he had dug up the body of his own wife.

In Prestonpans, just outside Edinburgh, another calamitous case is rumoured to have occurred, not long before the Anatomy Act was passed. Two resurrection men keen to get their hands on a cadaver described to them as a 'plump subject', set about digging with earnest. The mother of one of the men had recently died of cholera and had also been buried in Prestonpans. In fact, she had been buried in the grave next to the one they were enthusiastically attacking. It does not take much imagination to guess what happened next.

The bodysnatcher's mother was mistakenly disinterred and hastily reburied. This unfortunate event does have a twist in the tale. The two bodysnatchers were seized with cholera the next day and by the evening both had died. They were buried the following morning, alongside the grave they had recently disturbed.

During the first few decades of the nineteenth century, bodysnatching was thrust into the public limelight. Stories appeared in the press far more often than people would have wished and even the faintest rumour of a bodysnatcher being in the vicinity could result in public outcry. By the end of 1829, following the hanging of one half of the notorious murderers Burke and Hare, the term 'Burking' began to be used by the press and public alike to describe any form of attempted kidnap or murder. The pair, also known as 'The Westport Murderers', would suffocate their victims before delivering them to the very appreciative Dr Knox at No. 10 Surgeons Square, Edinburgh.

Towards the end of 1831, the 'London Burkers' had also been discovered and the crimes of John Bishop, Thomas Williams and James May would be the last straw for many. In 1824, the *Morning Chronicle* included a report from the *Evening Press* of a plasterer who had supposedly been 'stowed in a box like so much kippered salmon and driven off towards Berwick'. The plasterer was only found when the coach broke down at Carron, near Falkirk. When the paper ran the story the article 'expressed some grave doubts as to the truth of [it]' and quite rightly so, for it turned out that the apparent victim had used the tale to explain away some scars on his face which he had received 'in adventures of a very different description'.

But what was also evident in the article was the bad feeling towards Edinburgh University, which the paper described as possessing one of the best medical schools in the Empire. Yet, the article then stated that the medical school was 'now in a fair way to be the worst. The only dissection now practised in Edinburgh is the dissection of character'. This was five years before the Burke and Hare scandal of 1829, but public feeling towards bodysnatchers and the medical profession was already coloured with fear and disappointment, and it would only deteriorate further.

Burking hoaxes were often reported in the newspapers but the public's fear of the bodysnatchers raiding the churchyard in which their loved ones were buried was mounting, exacerbated by the exposure of high profile bodysnatchers. The authorities could no longer ignore just how prolific this activity had become. Something needed to be done to stop this base occupation in its tracks and the solution for many was the 1832 Anatomy Act, by which surgeons could take possession of the unclaimed dead from the parish workhouses.

However, even with the passing of this legislation, the fear that the bodies of those who had died of particularly unusual afflictions would still be desired by the anatomists was not easy to shake. When 'Mr F' 'consigned one of his children to the house appointed for all living' in a churchyard in Dewsbury, West Yorkshire in 1838, he was certain that the bodysnatchers would come to take his beloved child away. It was widely known that the child had died of a peculiar disease which would have made their corpse desirable to the surgeons.

Determined not to let anything untoward happen to his child, 'Mr F' decided to sit and watch the grave. Visiting the nearest inn and 'supplying himself with sufficient of that which makes Dutchmen courageous'; he was then given a gun and a brace of pistols by the inn keeper and set off to the graveyard. 'Mr F' did not have to wait too long, for he soon saw 'a form tall and ghastly standing motionless over the new opened grave'. Retreating in order to get assistance, 'Mr F' returned to the scene only to find that the 'form' was now bent forward over the grave. 'Mr F' fired a volley of bullets and was about to release some more when his companion suddenly stopped him. The would-be resurrectionist turned out to be a horse that had made its way into the churchyard.

Finally, in 1820 the *Caledonian Mercury* reported the following story:

> 'We mentioned in our last that the head of a man had been found by some labourers in Hyde Park, opposite St George's Hospital: it has since been ascertained to be that of John Saunders, who formerly held the position of porter in the above hospital where after a lingering illness he died of consumption, and was buried in the burial ground of the hospital at Brompton. It is supposed that some resurrection men placed the head in the above position.'

The eighteenth and nineteenth century newspapers were not afraid to include the more gruesome of details of bodysnatchers' antics. With the stories of Burke and Hare about to grace the pages of newspapers across the nation, perhaps it was best that people were already becoming hardened to these dark tales.

Chapter Nine

The Final Chapter
Bodysnatching at the time of the Anatomy Act

'A copy of the new Bill, which has just been brought into Parliament for the avowed purpose of doing away with the disgusting practices and horrible atrocities which have hitherto attended . . . has been published'
– Derby Mercury Wednesday, 28 December 1831.

In December 1842, James Allen, Secretary of the York School of Medicine, wrote a letter to Northallerton Workhouse in North Yorkshire, requesting more cadavers in accordance with the recently passed Anatomy Act. The bodies, he explained, were intended for the 'purpose of anatomical instruction' and Mr Allen wanted to make use of 'the unclaimed dead . . . the present supply for the school being insufficient'.

By this time York School of Medicine was in desperate need of bodies. The School's usual sources, the Castle Hospital and the County Hospital, could not keep up with their requirements so they wanted the newly passed Anatomy Act to deliver what it had promised. The Leeds and Sheffield Schools of Anatomy, Allen's letter noted, 'obtained several [cadavers] from Wakefield House of Correction, there being a general order to the effect that all the unclaimed dead should be sent there.'

But how had the medical schools come to require so many bodies for anatomical demonstrations in the first place? From the mid-eighteenth century, dissection was considered an additional punishment for murderers, depriving them of a Christian burial. After the 1752 Murder Act, the bodies of those convicted of murder could be dissected by surgeons if this was included as part of their sentence. Very few god-fearing Britons wanted any part of it. Dissection was for criminals and no changes in the law or any amount of persuasion by the medical profession as to the benefits of donating your body to the surgeons after death, would alter things.

However, a few people did donate their bodies to science. Jeremy Bentham bequeathed his body to Dr Southwood Smith, who publicly dissected it following Bentham's death in June 1832. Bentham was subsequently preserved for perpetuity and can still be seen today, seated in a glass case in University College, London. But he was only one of a handful of people willing to hand over their bodies to the surgeons after death, and perhaps the actions of a London surgeon can help us to understand why.

In December 1817, the *Trewman's Flying Post* printed a small article under the heading 'A Strange Case'. The report centred on a request from a seaman who was asking for his mother's head back from 'some half-hearted fellows in the Borough'. A surgeon from St Thomas' Hospital in London had removed the woman's head after she had died following a toothache. The surgeon had graciously informed the seaman that 'they [the surgeons] were willing to let [him] do what [he] pleased with the body'. The seaman, although permitting the surgeons to dissect his mother's head, did not for one moment think that they would keep it once they had finished cutting and examining it.

Unable to settle, the seaman wanted to reunite his mother's head with the rest of her corpse, so he asked the surgeons for it back. They refused. It transpired that the seaman's father had in fact sold his wife's head to the surgeons at St Thomas' Hospital for the sum of one pound.

Tales in which attempts to raid surgeons' rooms to find a loved one before the anatomists wielded their scalpels were relatively common, and revealed the horrors of dissection to the world. Mutilated lips and mangled eyeballs discovered on dissecting room floors or in barrels and detached jaw bones with flesh still clinging to the bone, are just some of the finds reported in newspapers.

This perceived disregard for the deceased went little way to improve relations between the medical establishment and the populace. If that was how a corpse was treated, then this provided little encouragement to donate your body to the surgeons after death.

The majority of people, however, still agreed that to ensure the advancement of medicine it was vital that students had at least some anatomical knowledge. The Anatomy Act stated that the study of anatomy was imperative to ensure the 'healing and repairing of divers wounds'. Those passing sentence on the bodysnatchers who were unlucky enough to find themselves standing in the dock, often showed their understanding of the inadequate supply of cadavers for the anatomy schools.

After Robert Armstrong and Thomas Stewart were arrested in 1824 for stealing the bodies of Martha Goodwin and Philip Hayes from St John's Church in Liverpool, the magistrate sentencing the pair felt the need to express his own opinion on the lack of cadavers available for dissection. He felt 'that it was necessary for the improvement of anatomical science that subjects should be procured' – a brave statement, considering that there were over one hundred angry parishioners waiting outside the court room.

A petition regarding the imprisonment of Armstrong and Stewart, signed by thirty-six members of the Liverpool Literary and Philosophical Society, was sent to the Treasury in 1826. The petition stated that 'it is for the public interest that professors of Medicine and Surgery should have scientific knowledge of Anatomy'. It also clearly highlighted the consequences of the current legislation regarding the legal supply of cadavers: 'the disinterment of dead bodies for the purpose of dissection is a necessary evil and must continue until some other mode is devised by legislation.'

In 1828, a Select Committee was appointed 'to enquire into the manner of obtaining subjects for dissection in the Schools of Anatomy'. Amongst those questioned were three bodysnatchers, one of whom is believed to have been the former gang leader Ben Crouch. Questions were asked about how many cadavers were procured and if, in his opinion, bodysnatching could be remedied by importing cadavers from abroad; the answer to which was 'doubtful'.

The Report highlighted the continuing difficulties surgeons had in procuring sufficient numbers of cadavers for their students. Price fluctuations and the inadequate numbers meant that alterations in the bodysnatching supply chain had to be made. The surgeons were more than happy to accept cadavers of the 'unclaimed' dead from the country's workhouses. After all this was how cadavers were acquired on the Continent and it seemed to be working over there. The result of the committee was unanimous: for medical knowledge to improve the number of cadavers available to the surgeons and anatomists would have to increase.

* * *

Burke and Hare are nearly always described as bodysnatchers. They sold their victims to an anatomist in Edinburgh, but that is where their link to bodysnatching ends. Not once did they take up a spade and exhume a corpse in the dead of night. We know of their story because it excited the populace like no other, bringing attention to the fact that there was a severe lack of cadavers available to the medical profession.

Based in West Port, Edinburgh, Burke and Hare began trading in corpses because they wanted to make some quick, easy money. They were successful for a short time, supplying Dr Knox at No. 10 Surgeons Square, Edinburgh with sixteen fresh subjects in total. But they became too blasé, too greedy for the large amounts of money that they could make from cadavers. They became less selective in choosing their victims. People were beginning to notice the disappearance of certain characters on the streets of Edinburgh and, when the anatomy students began to question the freshness of some of the cadavers, questions were asked about the pair.

Their career came to an abrupt end at the beginning of November 1828, when Ann and James Gray, lodgers at William Burke's house, became suspicious as to the whereabouts of their fellow lodger Madge Doherty. After searching high and low for Madge, the Gray's finally discovered her lifeless body under a bed. Hare turned King's evidence and was given immunity, but Burke was executed on 28 January 1829, his lifeless body receiving the same treatment as the subjects he had supplied to Dr Knox.

The actions of these two men did not stop the midnight forays of bodysnatchers up and down the county. Everyone knew that these raids were taking place; all Burke and Hare managed to do was to excite the populace further, and provide the public with a phrase that became synonymous with every attempted kidnapping and murder reported in the press. The term 'burking' was printed throughout newspapers up and down the land whenever a journalist decided to link the Edinburgh murders with a case elsewhere.

Though the act of 'burking' was probably minimal, henceforth, in order to excite the populace every assault involving someone being grabbed was presented in similar terms and the duo were immortalised for decades to come. In 1831 the *Leicester Chronicle* reported a case under the headline 'Daring Attempt to Burke a Child'. Eight-year-old Elizabeth Turner had been lured away from her front door in Waterloo Road, Queen Square, London by a man offering her a penny and sweetmeats. Needless to say, his intentions were unsavoury and Elizabeth, on being bound by her hands and feet, suffered a beating when she would not stop screaming. Her attacker then ran away when help appeared. No link to bodysnatching or surgeons was ever established.

The *Leicester Chronicle* reported another 'burking' case in the same edition. This time the young woman involved, Eliza Campbell, was walking down a lonely footpath between Union Street and Camden Street in London when she came upon a man lying across the path. When Eliza got near, the man jumped up and knocked her to the floor. Whilst 'endeavouring to stop her breath' another man appeared with a sack and the two struggled to seize Eliza. Her cries drew people to the scene, and the men escaped into the surrounding streets. Again, no connection to bodysnatching was established.

The matter of increasing the supply of cadavers to anatomists was raised in the House of Commons in 1831, when it was 'suggested that we [Britain] should exchange the manufactured goods of England for the dead bodies of France'. This, of course did not happen, but it was believed that if the British Government followed France's lead, 'there [would] be an end to Burking and body snatching.'

In France, surgeons were permitted the bodies of those poor souls who were found dead on the streets of Paris and could not be identified. They were also allowed to remove bodies found floating in the River Seine and, such was the availability of cadavers for the French teaching hospitals, that the anatomy school at La Pitié Hôpital, Paris estimated it received up to twelve cadavers per day, something that English and Scottish anatomists could only dream of.

Official acknowledgement that the medical profession was grossly under-supplied with cadavers, together with public anxiety and the knowledge that men were prepared to murder in order to provide subjects for the dissecting table had made bodysnatching a hot topic. The climax came in the winter of 1831, when the 'London Burkers', John Bishop, Thomas Williams and James May were tried for the murder of Carlo Ferrari, known as 'The Italian Boy'. Like William Burke, Bishop and Williams were sentenced to death and their bodies subsequently dissected, while May was reprieved.

A few days after Bishop and Williams were dissected, the Anatomy Act was heard in Parliament for a second time. The Act was designed to deliver an increased supply of cadavers to anatomy schools by permitting surgeons the use the 'unclaimed dead' from the workhouse, asylum or hospital. This was only granted once a full forty-eight hours had passed from their last breath. A certificate would then be issued stating the manner in which the person died, before the body was allowed to be passed to the surgeons for dissection.

The Act was finally passed on 11 May 1832, after a third and final reading, receiving Royal assent on 1 August 1832. The result was a devastating blow to the poor. If someone happened to die alone and unloved in an institution with no one to claim their body, regardless of their wishes, they would be sent to the surgeons for dissection.

This move was naturally resented and feared. Dissection was still very much linked with punishment for murder and many felt that it was simply not right for innocent people to be subjected to a punishment handed out to convicted felons.

In December 1833, 'considerable excitement among the populace of [Cambridge]' was caused by the local anatomy school having procured the body of a pauper for dissection. The body in question belonged to a Mr Porter, who was thought to have rented a house in Trinity Parish. On becoming ill, he had applied to the parish for relief until he could be removed to his own parish in Lincolnshire. Mr Porter did not recover and subsequently passed away, so the anatomy school claimed his body. Problems began to occur when it was discovered that the anatomy school in Cambridge had not gone down the correct route in order to secure Porter's body for dissection.

Unbeknownst to everyone in Cambridge, Mr Porter had relatives in his home parish of Lincolnshire, who could therefore have claimed his body. A 300-strong mob made their way to the anatomy school after this was discovered. Stones were thrown at the windows, which in turn smashed specimen jars lined up on shelves nearby; the crowd shouted each time a fresh noise of shattering glass could be heard.

The doors of the medical school had been forced open just before the Riot Act was read out to the mob and further destruction of the premises continued. All this damage was the result of a body being illegally acquired through a misunderstanding. The populace was clearly unhappy about the treatment of the 'unclaimed dead' under the new legislation and would not tolerate any perceived abuse of the system.

While the supply increased, the demand for corpses did not slow down once the Anatomy Act came into force. Bodysnatchers did not go out of business overnight. Orders still had to be met, students and anatomists had to be supplied. Although the number of bodysnatching cases reported in the press reduced dramatically, the old methods of procuring cadavers continued to be used.

In April 1832, just as the Anatomy Act was being discussed in Parliament, a case often described as the last arrest of a bodysnatcher in England occurred. William (Bill) Hollis was caught red-handed with two dead bodies in a cart, while making his way down New Cross Road in London. The bodies were those of two convicts who had died on the prison hulks a week previous.

Hollis was by no means the last convicted bodysnatcher. Snatchings throughout England and Scotland appeared spasmodically in the newspapers for many years after the Act was passed. In 1862, Sheffield sexton Isaac Howard was arrested when it was discovered that he had been disinterring bodies from Wardsend Cemetery and selling them to Sheffield Medical School. When testing the ground during the planning of a new vault for a corner of the cemetery, a large number of empty coffins were discovered during the excavations. Whilst some of the coffins 'contained no corpses . . . there were portions of flesh, which appeared to have been trodden under foot' around the area, with 'one body [having] evidently been cut to pieces and packed in a square box'. It was presumed that the box contained a dissected body waiting re-interment.

Parishioners gathering in the cemetery the following day were faced with a grisly scene. Standing around the excavation site, one by one the growing crowd covered their faces with handkerchiefs, as the stench was so bad. The hole in which the coffins were found had been dug into the side of a hill and measured roughly 12ft by 8ft. The coffins were in a terrible jumbled state, some covered with stones and others with soil.

It was estimated that there were about twelve coffins in total and these included the coffins of stillborn infants. Nearly all of the lids from the coffins had been removed. Adult remains were discovered at one end of the hole and although most of the coffins were empty, the 'outline features of one of the children was distinctly traceable, though the eyes and lips were gone, and a lock of hair still lay curled upon the forehead', according to the newspaper report.

Howard was arrested and later sentenced to three months' imprisonment. Yet, in some respects he profited from his time in prison. When the discovery was first made at the cemetery, a mob had gathered and had made their way to Howard's house, subsequently emptying it of his furniture and burning it down. The value of the destroyed items, together with the cost of damage sustained to his premises during the raid was calculated to be around five hundred pounds. Howard was awarded the sum of two hundred pounds from the county for the replacement of his goods.

Sextons were not alone in wrongdoing, however. Anatomists were also responsible for keeping their old supply routes open. In September 1832, not long after the passing of the Anatomy Act, William Sands Cox, a lecturer at Birmingham Medical School, entered into correspondence with an N. Somerville from the Office of Inspector of Anatomy. In the letters that passed between the two gentlemen, discussions referred to a resurrectionist who had offered a dead body to the Birmingham Medical School, an act which Sands Cox subsequently reported to the authorities.

Somerville congratulated Sands Cox on providing 'the strongest proof of the determination of the teachers to put down illegal practices', for, he said, 'it would be a real source of grief to us all that the abominable practices should be revived, especially at Birmingham'. In November, Sands Cox received another letter from Somerville, who noted that he had 'accidently omitted to insert a name of the person from whom [he'd] received the body'.

Sands Cox may have left the name of the resurrectionist out of his letter but Somerville was still carrying out investigations in London and had already questioned two resurrectionists to find out who they were employed by. No names are given in the letters, but Somerville writes that one resurrectionist stated, 'that he was given an order from Birmingham, and that the body had to be forwarded to Mr Dunn'. Somerville seems to have believed that Sands Cox was somehow involved in this affair.

It was impractical to expect transactions between surgeons and resurrection men to suddenly stop overnight. Anatomists' demands for fresh cadavers had not diminished, so why would bodysnatchers stop working? Many bodysnatchers did go out of business as a result of the Act, whilst some opportunists could not resist exhuming a corpse for the surgeons, as a late case reported in the *Lloyds Weekly Newspaper* towards the end of April 1849 shows.

After suffering a long illness, Mr Robert Brown's son had passed away. Mr Brown's servants, feeling unsettled after the burial, took it in turns to watch over the recently filled grave. They were quite right to have concerns for when the groom was keeping watch, he saw 'two or three men in the churchyard, busily employed' actually throwing soil out of the grave. When the groom approached the men, they had 'got to the depth of about two spades'. The groom threatened the bodysnatchers with a gun, but he was not prepared to have one turned on himself. Luckily, the bodysnatcher was a poor shot and the bullet missed.

The groom immediately fired back and shot the bodysnatcher in the chest. Thinking that he had wounded the bodysnatcher, or even killed him, the groom went for assistance. On his return, all that was left of the trio of bodysnatchers was a trail of blood leading out of the churchyard and into the distance.

* * *

The drive and determination of eighteenth and nineteenth century anatomists to discover the secrets of the human body has led to medical innovations that far outweigh what was once thought possible. Any solution to supplying the anatomy schools of England and Scotland with sufficient numbers of cadavers was always going to be controversial. The Anatomy Act was an attempt to make up this shortfall, in the hope that not only would it help furnish the dissecting tables of England and Scotland, but it would also put an immediate stop to the despicable behaviour of Britain's bodysnatchers.

Neither of these aims can be classed as wholly immediately successful, as the number of cadavers made available by the new legislation were small. Extensive research carried out by Ruth Richardson, in her renown work *Death, Dissection and the Destitute*, shows that in the first year following the passing of the Act nearly 400 cadavers were taken from parish workhouses by anatomists.

When James Allen, Secretary of the York School of Medicine wrote to Northallerton Workhouse in 1842, requesting the use of their 'unclaimed dead', Richardson's research shows that during the same year only 216 cadavers were taken from workhouses across the country. Medical student numbers at this time have been estimated at about 270 in London alone and, considering the total number of students nationwide, there was still a huge shortfall. A year later, Richardson's research shows that the total number of bodies obtained by anatomists from institutions had risen to 378.

The role of the bodysnatcher certainly did not cease on 2 August 1832, the day after the Act was passed. The resurrection business rumbled on in the background; newspapers reporting periodically on nervous parishioners guarding the graves of their loved ones and the determined bodysnatcher still supplying the anatomists with a fresh cadaver or two. For nearly one hundred years, members of every parish in England and Scotland had lived in fear of the bodysnatcher and some parishes were a little reluctant to give up their churchyard surveillance completely.

In a few cases their suspicions were proved right. An arrest was made in St Pancras Church, London, in 1849 as a result of one respectable gentleman keeping watch over the grave of his recently buried niece. Watching over the grave of a loved one was not illegal and the man in question, Mr Harwood of Norton Green, was doing nothing wrong. What was alarming, however, was the fact that he was armed with a gun and a 'chopper' (presumably an axe).

When questioned, it transpired that Mr Harwood had a strong suspicion that his niece's remains 'would be disturbed by bodysnatchers for the surgeons'. He was later discharged but this case shows how the actions of the resurrection men had become ingrained into society even after legislation had been passed to remedy the situation.

As the years passed however, many of the resurrection men simply moved on to some other illegal occupation, such as coining or burglary. Others, like Joseph Naples, turned their hand to respectable trades. Naples put the skills he had picked up as a bodysnatcher to good use, gaining employment in the dissecting rooms at St Thomas' Hospital, London.

Some bodysnatchers fell into even less salubrious occupations. In April 1833, former bodysnatcher William Drinkley was charged with counterfeiting 'two crown-pieces' at the Middlesex Sessions and sentenced to one year's imprisonment. In the same year, bodysnatcher Patrick Fitzgerald was charged with assault after he was challenged by a female shopkeeper for not paying his debts: clear evidence that he was in need of funds with his previous income now cut off. With no honest occupation to return to after the Anatomy Act came into force, many resurrection men had little alternative but to turn to other forms of crime to survive.

Today, many people willingly donate their bodies to science in an attempt to help doctors to understand the development of modern diseases. Without the help of the now mostly forgotten resurrection men, one has to question the speed at which our understanding of the human body would have progressed. Without the determination of anatomists to understand what truly lay beneath the skin of the human body, one has to wonder how quickly our understanding would have moved away from the misconceptions of the Greek anatomist Galen.

Bibliography

Titles relating specifically to bodysnatching:

Abbott, Geoffrey, *Grave Disturbances: A History of the Body Snatchers* (Eric Dobby Publishing, 2006).

Adams, Norman, *Dead and Buried: The Horrible History of Bodysnatching* (Bell Publishing Company, n.d).

Adams, Norman, *Scottish Bodysnatchers: True Accounts* (Goblinshead, 2002).

Bailey, Brian, *The Resurrection Men: A History of the Trade in Corpses* (Macdonald, 1991).

Bailey, James Blake, *Diary of a Resurrectionist 1811-1812, To Which Are Added an Account of the Resurrection Men in London and a Short History of the Passing of the Anatomy Act* (Accessed via www.gutenberg.org).

Ball, James Moores, *The Body Snatchers: Doctors, Grave Robbers and the Law* (Dorset Press, 1989).

Ball, James Moores, *Sack -'Em-Up Men': An Account of the Rise and Fall of The Modern Resurrectionists* (Oliver and Boyd, 1928).

Cole, Hubert, *Things for the Surgeon: A History of the Resurrection Men* (Heinemann, 1964).

Drimmer, Fredrick, *The Body Snatchers: Stiffs and Other Ghoulish Delights* (Citadel Press, 1992).

Fido, Martin, *Bodysnatchers: A History of the Resurrectionists 1742-1832* (Weidenfield & Nicolson, 1988).

Fowler, L, Powers, N, *Doctors, Dissection and Resurrection Men: Excavations in the 19th Century Burial Ground of the London Hospital, 2006* (Museum of London Archaeology, 2012).

Holder, Geoff, *Scottish Bodysnatchers: A Gazetteer* (The History Press, 2010).

Ramsey, Ted, *Don't Walk Down College Street* (Ramshorn, 1985).

Richardson, Ruth, *Death, Dissection and the Destitute: The Politics of the Corpse in Pre-Victorian Britain* (Phoenix Press, 2001).

Salkeld, Marjorie, 'A Body in a Gig in Charles Street' in *Collected Articles from The Bulletin of East Yorkshire Local History Society*, Nos 1-155, 1970 – Feb 1997, Volume 2, Authors M-Z.

Wise, Sarah, *The Italian Boy: Murder and Grave-Robbery in 1830's London* (Jonathan Cape, 2004).

General medical history titles:

Burch, Druin, *Digging Up The Dead: Uncovering the Life and Times of an Extraordinary Surgeon* (Chatto & Windus, 2007).

Moore, Wendy, *The Knife Man* (Bantam Press, 2005).

Pattison, F.L.M, *Granville Sharp Pattison: Anatomist and Antagonist 1791-1851* (Canongate, 1987).

Regency Library, *Memorials: John Flint South - Introduction By Robert Gittings* (Centaur Press Ltd, 1970).

Local and social history titles:

Andrews, William, *Beyond England: Social Studies in its Historic Byways & Highways* (1892).

Arnold, Catherine, *Necropolis: London & Its Dead* (Simon & Schuster UK Ltd, 2006).

Campbell, Marie, *Curious Tales of Old West Yorkshire* (Sigma Leisure, 1999).

Cobbett, William, *'Cobbett's Political Register Volume.75'* (Cox & Baylis, 1831) (Accessed via http://tinyurl.com/qzau6rs).

Eadon Leader, Robert, *Reminiscences of Old Sheffield* (Leader & Sons, Sheffield, 1876).

Hawkins, David. T, *Criminal Ancestors: A Guide to Historical Criminal Records in England and Wales* (The History Press, 2009).

MacLeod, Donald, *God's Acres of Dumbarton* (T. Murray & Son, Glasgow, 1888) (Accessed via http://www.geograph.org.uk/article/Dumbarton-Cemetery# proposals)

Marshall, John, *The Annals of Yorkshire from the Earliest Period to the Present Time* (Crosby, 1852) (Accessed via http://tinyurl.com/qyffjod).

Peach, Howard, *Curious Tales of Old East Yorkshire* (Sigma Leisure, 2001).

Peach, Howard, *Curious Tales of Old North Yorkshire* (Sigma Leisure, 2004).

Story, Neil R., *A Grim Almanac of Cambridgeshire* (History Press, 2009).

Sykes, John, *Local Records or Historical Register of Remarkable Events which have occurred in Northumberland and Durham , Newcastle-upon-Tyne and Berwick-upon-Tweed: Volume II*, Newcastle, 1833 (Patrick& Shotton, 1973).

Wade, Stephen, *Tracing Your Criminal Ancestors: A Guide to Family Historians* (Pen & Sword, 2009).

Research Sources

Newspapers:

References to bodysnatching, and later 'burking' appear in various newspapers throughout the period and beyond. The newspapers mentioned here are an example of those most often used.

Aberdeen Evening Press – 1887.
Berkshire Chronicle – 1828.
Berrow's Worcester Journal – 1822.
Berwickshire News and General Advertiser – 1906.
Bristol Mercury – 1827.
Bury and Norwich Post – 1817, 1823, 1829, 1831, 1849.
Caledonian Mercury – 1739, 1742, 1802, 1817, 1819, 1820, 1821, 1825, 1826.
Cambridge Chronicle and Journal – 1825, 1827, 1830.
Chester Chronicle – 1816, 1825, 1828.
Coventry Herald – 1833.
Derby Mercury – 1815, 1827.
Devises and Wilshire Gazette – 1822, 1823.
Durham County Advertiser – 1820, 1828.
Exeter and Plymouth Gazette – 1827.
Freeman's Journal – 1831.
Glasgow Herald – 1821, 1822, 1874.
Glasgow Chronicle – 1822.
Hampshire Chronicle – 1820, 1825, 1826, 1827.
Hampshire Telegraph – 1825.
Hereford Journal – 1832.
Hue and Cry – 1817, 1818.
Hull Advertiser – 1832, 1834.
Hull Packet – 1817, 1826, 1832, 1833, 1834.
Huntingdon, Bedford and Peterborough Gazette – 1831.
Ipswich Journal – 1796, 1818, 1823.
Jackson's Oxford Journal – 1810, 1818, 1821, 1823, 1830, 1831.
Lancaster Gazette – 1826, 1831.
Leeds Intelligencer – 1826, 1831, 1832.

Leeds Mercury – 1824, 1826, 1829, 1831, 1832.
Leeds Times – 1833, 1838.
Leicester Chronicle – 1827, 1831.
Liverpool Mercury – 1823, 1824, 1826, 1828.
London Daily News – 1849.
Lloyds Weekly Newspaper – 1849.
Manchester Guardian – 1831.
Manchester Mercury – 1817, 1828.
Morning Chronicle – 1817, 1822, 1823, 1824, 1825, 1826, 1827, 1828, 1829, 1832.
Morning Post – 1811, 1818, 1821, 1822, 1823, 1826, 1827, 1828, 1829, 1831, 1832.
Newcastle Chronicle – 1782.
Newcastle Courant – 1742, 1792, 1829, 1830.
Nottinghamshire Guardian – 1862.
Oxford Journal – 1759, 1765, 1776.
Oracle and Public Advertiser – 1798.
Preston Chronicle – 1831.
Royal Worcester Gazette – 1830.
Salisbury and Winchester Journal – 1825.
Sheffield Independent – 1830, 1831, 1832.
Stamford Mercury – 1816, 1823, 1827, 1830.
Sunday Reformer and Universal Register – 1795.
Sussex Advertiser – 1827.
Taunton Courier – 1827, 1830.
The Era – 1849.
The Examiner – 1822, 1828.
The Observer – 1832.
The Scots Magzine – 1742.
The Standard – 1828, 1830, 1831.
The Times – 1815, 1819, 1826.
The Universal Magazine – 1796.
Trewman's Exeter Flyer – 1832.
Western Daily Press – 1862.
Western Mail – 1869.
Westmoreland Gazette – 1824.
York Gazette – 1826, 1831.
York Herald – 1826, 1827, 1828, 1829, 1831, 1832.
Yorkshire Gazette – 1831, 1832.

Online Resources:

Durr, Peter, 'The Little Leighs Body Snatchers'
(Accessed via www.essex.police.uk/museum/historynotebooks/51.pdf).

Martyn Gorman, 'Echos of the Resurrection Men'
(Accessed via www.abdn.ac.uk/bodysnatchers/index.php).

Report from the Select Committee on Anatomy, 1828
(Accessed via www.archive.org/stream/reportfromselect00grea#page/10/
mode/2up

Smith Jnr., Richard, *A History of the Bristol Royal Infirmary*, 1917
(Accessible via Internet Archive: http://archive.org/stream/historyofbristol00
smit/historyofbristol00smit_djvu.txt)

Victorian County History, *A History of the County of Middlesex Vol II: Stepney
& Bethnal Green* (Accessible via www.british-history.ac.uk/vch/middx/vol1)

Archives:
University of Aberdeen Special Collections

The university holds the records for the Aberdeen Medico-Chirurgical Society,
which includes minute books recording bodysnatching activity in AMCS/1:
Institutional Records.

University of Aberdeen Special Collections
Special Collections Centre,
The Sir Duncan Rice Library,
Bedford Road,
Aberdeen,
AB24 3AA
Tel: 01224 272598
Website: www.abdn.ac.uk/library

The Bodleian Library

The John Johnson Collection is a collection of printed ephemera, available to
view online and mainly covers the eighteenth to early twentieth centuries.

Bodleian Library,
Broad Street,
Oxford,
OX1 3BG
Tel: 01865 277162
Website: www.bodleian.ox.ac.uk/johnson/about

The British Newspaper Archive

This website provides online access to over seven million digitised newspaper pages from the British Library collection, with new editions being frequently added. Many articles relating to bodysnatching and the feelings surrounding the Anatomy Act can be found, as well as general news articles and advertisements.

Website: www.britishnewspaperarchive.co.uk

The National Archives

The National Archives hold petitions in series HO17, as well as the Criminal Register of England & Wales in series HO26 and HO27. Papers relating to John Craig Hodgson can be found in ASSI 44 and ASSI 45.

The National Archives,
Kew,
Richmond,
Surrey TW9 4DU
Tel: 02088 763444
Website: www.nationalarchives.gov.uk

The National Archives of Scotland

Cases relating to bodysnatching can be found for various years in the Crown Office Precognitions in series AD14. The Precognition against Henry Gillies (AD 14/28/207) as well as trial papers (JC26/1828/234) are held here. The NAS online catalogue is available at: www.nrscotland.gov.uk/research/catalogues-and-indexes

The National Archives of Scotland,
H M General Register House,
2 Princes Street,
Edinburgh,
EH1 3YY
Tel: 01315 351314
Website: www.nas.gov.uk

National Library of Scotland

The website 'Word on the Street' run by the National Library of Scotland has over 1800 broadsides available to view online, with many relating to bodysnatching.

Naturally, a large number of items relate to the West Port murderers Burke and Hare. The broadsides can be viewed at www.digital.nls.uk/broadsides

National Library of Scotland
George IV Bridge,
Edinburgh,
EH1 1EW
Tel: 01316 233700
Website: www.nls.uk

Newgate Calendar

The Newgate Calendar contains a wealth of information relating to the dark underworld of Georgian Britain, although little in the way of bodysnatching cases. Originally a compilation of broadsides focusing on the trials of notorious criminals, the Calendar covers the period 1824 and 1826 and provides a wealth of information when researching criminals.

Website: www.exclassics.com/newgate/ngintro.htm

Old Bailey Online

This online collection covers the proceedings of the Old Bailey, from 1674–1913 and includes 197,745 criminal trials held at London's central criminal court. A limited number of bodysnatchers are mentioned and usually in relation to some other crime.

Website: www.oldbaileyonline.org

Royal College of Surgeons, London

One of the most valuable of resources to have survived from the macabre era of bodysnatching is the 'Diary of a Resurrectionist' believed to be written by Joseph Naples. It can be found in series MS0024. Due to the fragile nature of the Diary it can only be viewed as an electronic copy in the College's Reading Room.

Website: www.rcseng.ac.uk/museums/archives

Tracing a Bodysnatcher
Through the Archives

Unless you already know the name of a particular bodysnatcher then it can be quite laborious searching through the records of the Quarter Sessions or Calendar of Prisoners available at county archives.

Your research should begin with newspapers, in which information relating to a trial will be given. This can help to narrow down your search and reduce the time you'll spend searching in the archives. Online catalogues are increasingly becoming available from archives across the country and, although specific details may not be viewed online, details about holdings can often be obtained.

The archives and online catalogues for local archives and record offices consulted during the research for this book include:

Bedfordshire & Luton Archives Gaol Database

Bedfordshire and Luton Archives and Records Service
Riverside Building
Borough Hall
Bedford
MK42 9AP
Tel: 01234 228833
Website: http://apps.bedfordshire.gov.uk/grd

Essex County Record Office

Wharf Rd,
Chelmsford,
Essex,
CM2 6YT
Tel: 01245 244615
Website: http://seax.essexcc.gov.uk

Huntingdonshire Archives & Local Studies

Prince's St,
Huntingdon,
Cambridgeshire,
PE29 3PA
Tel: 03450 455225
Website: http://tinyurl.com/pubkqu3

North Yorkshire County Record Office

Malpas Road
Northallerton
North Yorkshire
DL7 8TB
Tel: 01609 777585
Website: www.northyorks.gov.uk/article/23584/County-record-office

West Yorkshire Archive Service

WYAS, Wakefield office
Registry of Deeds
Newstead Road
Wakefield
WF1 2DE
Tel: 01924 305980
Website: www.archives.wyjs.org.uk

Index